Paranormal
WEST
YORKSHIRE

Paranormal
WEST
YORKSHIRE

ANDY OWENS

The
History
Press

For Royston and Barbara Breeze
(and the wise Revd Perkins)

First published 2008

The History Press Ltd
The Mill, Brimscombe Port
Stroud, Gloucestershire, GL5 2QG
www.thehistorypress.co.uk

British Library Cataloguing in Publication Data.
A catalogue record for this book is available from the British Library.

ISBN 978 0 7524 4810 7

Typesetting and origination by The History Press Ltd.
Printed in Great Britain

CONTENTS

FOREWORD

When I first began research for this book, I worried that there may not be enough material purely in West Yorkshire to make an entire volume. How wrong I was! This west section of Yorkshire is positively brimming with mysteries of one kind or another.

As a big fan of Sherlock Holmes, I was fascinated to discover the foibles of his creator Sir Arthur Conan Doyle – a fervent believer in the Cottingley Fairies.

The notion that there are big cats prowling the countryside, only occasionally spotted by the public, is both intriguing and quite frightening. What would you do if, rambling over a hill in the middle of nowhere, you were faced with a wild animal, blocking your path, growling and snarling? Big-cat expert Paul Westwood offers a wealth of sensible advice. As far as I know there exists no photographic evidence of such a creature in Yorkshire. But then, if we are honest, how many of us are in the habit of carrying cameras with us from day to day? Strange things usually happen to people who are not seeking them.

The intriguing, horrific and mysterious death of Zigmund Adamski led me to appeal for information throughout Yorkshire and further afield, and although I was contacted by many people ranging from those who knew Mr Adamski to psychics and mediums offering to help me find a solution, the case remains unsolved to this day – and probably always will.

Other intriguing encounters range from UFO sightings and alien abduction to the bizarre mystery of spontaneous human combustion, which in this case was even more bizarre since it involved two sisters, in separate locations, who burst into flames at exactly the same time!

The vast majority of paranormal encounters recorded here, however, concern ghosts, hauntings, spirits and poltergeists, and it is this subject which commands almost half of the book. I have concentrated exclusively on 'modern' accounts, rather than myths and folk tales. While I have liberally plundered the best ghostly tales from some of my previous books on the subject, there are many intriguing first-hand accounts too, as a result of appealing for experiences from the readers of West Yorkshire's newspapers.

Time and time again, I have met with people who are not, I am convinced, publicity-hungry charlatans, or simple-minded attention-seekers – but normal people, in every respect, who have witnessed things which are not currently understood, or even accepted, by our scientists.

Technically speaking, we see ghosts every night. Stars in the night sky are ghosts, for we are not perceiving them as they are now, but as they were millions of years ago. They may no longer exist – but to our eyes, they do. I often think that a more open and receptive mind would do our human race a world of good.

Finally, I would like to thank you for buying my book. I always feel very grateful and flattered when people fork out hard-earned money to purchase something I have written, instead of the latest international bestseller, and I sincerely hope that my efforts justify your investment.

Also, if you have had any sightings or experiences of strange phenomena, or simply have comments (good or bad!), please write to me c/o my publishers, as I would love to hear from you, and I could perhaps feature your story in a future volume. No doubt I will be writing books on ghosts until I become a ghost myself!

Now, let us begin our magical mystery tour of West Yorkshire!

Andy Owens,
West Yorkshire, 2008.

ACKNOWLEDGEMENTS

I would like to thank everyone who contacted me to recount their experiences, and all those in libraries and tourist information centres who answered my many questions.

Particular thanks must go to all those who allowed me interviews, including Dawn Stead of Haunted Yorkshire Psychical Research and Paul Westwood of Big Cat Monitors; extra thanks to Paul for the loan of the graphic design from his website, and for arranging for me to reproduce the big cat photograph taken by Philip Grey as featured on www.bigcatmonitors.co.uk; also to Margaret Ludkin for her spooky photograph of Bolling Hall. Thanks also to Susanne Kittlinger of the Science & Society Picture Library for the Cottingley Fairy photograph. I would also like to thank Paul Napier, editor of the *Yorkshire Evening Post* and Susan Darrow, editor of *Psychic News,* for allowing me to reproduce the articles about my media appeals; plus Tony Ortzen and Andrew Hutchinson for the original interviews. Particular thanks to Cate Ludlow, Beth Hall and all at the History Press, for giving me the opportunity to write a second spooky volume for them, following *Haunted Bradford.*

one

THE PONTEFRACT
POLTERGEIST

The case of the Enfield Poltergeist is widely considered to be the most notorious case of poltergeist activity in Britain. The case is considered a classic in the history of psychical research, due to both the wide range of phenomena reported and the multitude of eyewitnesses to the events.

However, there was one Yorkshire case, also wide-ranging with multiple witnesses, which was almost forgotten. The Black Monk of Pontefract was only rescued from obscurity by a local historian who notified author Colin Wilson, who in turn investigated the case and devoted a chapter about it in his classic book, *Poltergeist: A Study in Destructive Haunting*.

At No. 30 East Drive, situated on the Chequerfields housing estate, in Pontefract, West Yorkshire, a plethora of poltergeist phenomena was reported by the Pritchard family. It began in August 1966, ended the next year and, after a break of two years, began again.

The Chequerfields housing estate is situated on a hill overlooking the ancient town, and the house in question stands very close to the site of the old gallows, where hundreds of people were executed. It also stands on a corner of the street; the exact spot where an old bridge used to span a small stream – the full significance of which will be explained later.

At the time, the resident family of four were Joe and Jean Pritchard, their son Phillip (aged fifteen) and their daughter Diane (aged twelve). At the start of the phenomena, Mr and Mrs Pritchard had gone on holiday to Devon, with Diane, leaving Phillip at home with his grandma, Mrs Scholes.

On the day the haunting began, Mrs Scholes was sitting knitting in the lounge, while Phillip was in the garden reading a book, enjoying the sunny day. A sudden wind stole through the house, rattling the windows and making the door slam shut. When Phillip came in, his gran asked if it had become windy outside, to which the boy replied that it was still very calm. Phillip offered to make them both a drink and he went to the kitchen. Ten minutes passed, and the lad brought the drinks into the lounge – and stopped dead.

A grey-white powder, like chalk dust, was floating gently down through the air, all around his grandma, who was so engrossed in her knitting that she had not noticed it. She looked up at Phillip and said, 'What have you been up to?'

'Nothing. I've been in the kitchen all the time. What is it?'

Everything in the room was covered in the dust and the two peered up at the ceiling wondering where it was coming from. The family had only recently papered the ceiling and they thought that the whitewash must be disintegrating – that is, until they realised that the white powder wasn't coming from the ceiling. When they stood up, they could see that a few inches below the ceiling was totally clear of the powder; it was materialising – and falling – from nowhere.

At this point they were not alarmed, only confused. Mrs Scholes thought the powder must have blown in from outside, but the theory did not make sense at all. However, it was the only logical conclusion they could think of for such an illogical happening.

Mrs Scholes went to fetch her daughter Marie Kelly and her husband ,Vic, who lived in the house directly opposite. Later, Marie recalled her astonishment when her mother entered her house covered in the dust from head to toe, and 'looking like a snowman'.

When they returned to the house, the powder was still falling and Marie Kelly was also dumbfounded. She quickly shook herself and said simply, 'We'd better get it cleaned up.' She went to the kitchen to get a cloth and slipped on a pool of water on the floor. So she got a mop and wiped it up but, every time she did so, she discovered another pool of water, and another, and another, all forming on the linoleum. She lifted up one corner and pulled it back, thinking there may have been a burst pipe, but the floor below was completely dry. An official from the Water Board also checked for leaking or damaged pipes and, clutching for straws, eventually suggested it was condensation which had formed due to the clammy weather, though the others knew this was preposterous. The weather had been completely dry for some time.

Enid Pritchard came in to see if she could help. She turned off the water supply, but the pools of water continued to appear. Also, when taps were turned on, and the toilet flushed, a greenish foam rushed out. About an hour later, the pools of water stopped appearing. However, at 7 p.m. that evening, Mrs Scholes and Phillip found the surface at the side of the kitchen sink was covered with sugar and dried tea leaves. And, as they watched, the button on the tea dispenser above the draining board went in and out of its own accord, dispensing tea.

A loud crash sent them hurrying to the hall, where they found a pot plant, usually kept at the foot of the stairs, in the middle step of the staircase: the pot itself had apparently leaped up to the landing. Back in the kitchen, the crockery cupboard was shaking and vibrating as if someone was locked in and trying to get out. Phillip opened the door and the vibrations stopped.

Mrs Scholes went to get her daughter again. When Marie Kelly arrived the crockery cupboard was shaking again. Although the husband of the next-door neighbour was a carpenter and could often be heard working on a project, the cupboard was on the end wall of the house – nothing was beyond it but the garden. Also, May Mountain, the next-door neighbour, denied making any noises; in fact, she thought it was them! They went to bed, even though the wardrobe in Phillip's bedroom also began 'tottering and swaying like a drunken man.'

At one point, the family invited a local vicar, the Revd Davy, along to the house to perhaps perform an exorcism. But the clergyman was unconvinced by the haunting. He sat in the house and listened to what the family told him but, after one-and-a-half hours, nothing had occurred. As he was about to leave, three loud thumps came from an upstairs bedroom and a small candlestick jumped off the mantelpiece onto the floor. Revd Davy scratched his head and suggested that their problems were down to subsidence. However, as he said this, another candlestick floated off the shelf, through the air, past the vicar's nose and dropped to the floor.

'Do you think that's subsidence?' asked Marie. As the vicar was about to speak there was a loud crash from the next room and they rushed in to find every cup, saucer and plate from the china cupboard had dropped to the floor – and yet none of them were broken or cracked.

This convinced Mr Davy that the phenomena was real. It was not explained why he did not offer an exorcism, but he warned that 'something evil' was in the house and advised the family to move. Jean Pritchard flatly refused to be driven from her home because of a ghost. And so the vicar left, but the family didn't, and there was no exorcism.

The family took to sleeping at the Kellys' house. They decided to call the police. An inspector named Taylor and two uniformed officers made a full search of the house and everything appeared to be normal. They returned to the station and the others returned to the Kellys' house. Vic said, 'What about your friend Mr O'Donald? He's interested in ghosts, isn't he?'

O'Donald came along to the house. As he entered he was met by a blast of cold air – which he described as like walking into a refrigerator. He explained that poltergeists usually centred on a person's unconscious, in this case probably Phillip's. 'They like doing funny things. They're very fond of tearing up photographs, I believe.' Vic said they were wasting their time, as Phillip was currently in their house. Mr O'Donald left. As the Kelly's were about to leave, there was a crash in the lounge. They found two small oil paintings lying on floor face downward. Glass shattered and a print in a frame – the wedding photograph of Joe and Jean Pritchard – had been slashed from end to end as if with a sharp knife. The poltergeist had apparently overheard Mr O'Donald.

When the family returned from their holiday all was at first quiet, and Mr Pritchard was sceptical of the reported poltergeist activity. 'What kind of knocks?' he asked. As if in reply, three loud, distinct bangs were heard, followed by a rattling of the window frames as a cold wind blew through the house. Silence fell; the temperature returned to normal. And there were no more disturbances for the next two years.

The peace, however, did not last: Jean and her mother were drinking tea during a break from redecorating Diane's room when Mrs Scholes said, 'I keep hearing noises.'

'Well, I don't and I'm in the house practically all the time,' Jean replied.

'Didn't you hear something then?'

'No,' said Jean and went to the hall. Later that day, strange things began to happen. She found a counterpane from her bed on the floor. She returned it, then a counterpane from Phillip's bed was there too, and a number of plant pots were upended on the carpet.

That night, Jean could not sleep. Even with both windows open the room was too warm. She went onto the landing. A paintbrush whizzed past her head, followed by a paste bucket scattering paste on the carpet. Both missed her and hit either side of the landing wall. In the dim light, she could see something moving. She switched on the light and saw a strip of a roll of wallpaper moving on its own. Bravely, she made a grab for it, and the paper fluttered gently to the floor.

The most frightening incident that occurred was when Diane was dragged up the stairs by an invisible force; her cardigan was stretched out in front of her as if someone was above her, with his other hand apparently around her throat. Phillip and Jean Pritchard began pulling her back down again and for a moment it seemed to be a tug-of-war match until the force finally let her go. Although shaken, and with red fingermarks evident on her throat, she was unhurt by the experience.

As the poltergeist haunting drew to an end, the family began to see what they assumed to be the poltergeist. Jean and Joe Pritchard were in bed one night when the door opened to reveal a tall figure in the doorway wearing a hood over its head. When they switched on the light, the figure had vanished.

A Spiritualist medium, Rene Holden, spent much time with the family. One night, as she was sitting with them in the lounge, the lights suddenly went out, and she felt a man's hand on the back of her head. As she glanced underneath her arm, she saw a long black garment, like a dressing gown (or indeed a monk's habit), as if someone was standing behind her, but when the lights came back on, there was no one there.

One day, whilst Phillip and Diane were watching television in the lounge, they glanced at the door, with its frosted glass, and saw a tall figure standing there. When Phillip opened the door, they were just in time to see the tall, black shape of a monk disappearing into the floor!

The haunting ended on the day the family took some advice from a friend to hang garlic in the house.

Colin Wilson points out that this was the method used in Dracula movies to keep vampires at bay! However, he suggests that the reason the poltergeist disappeared was because all of the family – including Phillip, the likely focus for the activity – were attempting to rid themselves of the presence. So it simply made its leave and never returned.

two

SPONTANEOUS HUMAN COMBUSTION

In their thorough, compelling and investigative book *Spontaneous Human Combustion*, Jenny Randles and Peter Hough relate a case of the phenomenon – and indeed the most bizarre case of spontaneous human combustion I have ever read – that occurred in Sowerby Bridge.

The authors found a press report from the *Halifax Evening Courier* dated Saturday 13 April 1985, in which the former editor, Edward Riley, refers to a case which occurred in 1899. I found the original newspaper account stored on microfiche. The happenings had been a closely guarded secret in the ninety-two years since its occurrence.

The Kirby family were Sara Ann and John Henry, and their daughters, five-year-old Alice Ann Kirby and four-year-old Amy Kirby (aged four), who all lived together in Sowerby Bridge.

Originally, the family lived on Hargreaves Terrace on London Road, until the parents separated. Although the two girls were still officially living at their mother's address, Alice went to live with her father and grandmother at No. 45 Wakefield Road.

Wakefield Road and London Road run parallel to one another, exactly a mile apart on opposite sides of the Calder Valley. The roads are linked by Fall Lane, which crosses the canal and the River Calder.

At 11 a.m. on Thursday 5 January 1899, Mrs Sara Kirby went outside Hargreave Terrace to get some water from the well, 20yds away. Because it was raining heavily, the task took no longer than two minutes. As she re-entered the house, she heard screams – and found Amy ablaze. Mrs Kirby told the inquest, 'If she had had paraffin oil thrown over her she would not have burned faster.'

Another witness claimed that flames a yard high were coming from the child's head. It was stated that Amy was afraid of fire and indeed there was no evidence of matches or charred paper. After it was all over, Mrs Kirby ran down Fall Lane to inform her husband of the tragedy. But, halfway across the valley, she was met by a messenger from her mother-in-law: Sara's other daughter, Alice, had been discovered on fire! The pair were reduced to tears and hysterics as they related their stories, which were virtually identical.

Grandmother Susan Kirby had left Alice in bed while she visited a neighbour. When she returned, she found the child '…enveloped in flames and almost burned to death.' There were no spent matches or burnt paper, and the fire in the grate had not been disturbed. The time was exactly 11 a.m.

Fall Lane, which links the two houses, running across the River Calder.

Wakefield Road, near Sowerby Bridge…

…and the view from London Road. The two houses are situated directly opposite each other across the valley.

Wakefield Road. (Courtesy of Stephen Gee)

Both girls were taken away in the same horse-drawn ambulance to the Royal Halifax Infirmary. Alice died at 3 p.m. that day, and Amy just before midnight.

Jenny Randles and Peter Hough relate that '…another of those strange name-related 'coincidences' seemingly endemic in spontaneous human combustion matters: the doctor who attended them both was Dr Wellburn.' From the authors' investigation into the subject, they pointed out how '…such synchronicities of name appear to be part of the alleged phenomenon.' An additional coincidence, which I found whilst taking photographs, is that the road just past the house off London Road is called Spark House Lane – weird!

Spontaneous human combustion was never mentioned at the inquest. Despite the lack of evidence, the coroner concluded that both deaths were an accident, and the jury agreed. But one juror admitted, 'we have no evidence to show how the fire occurred in either case.'

The coroner referred to the circumstances as 'strange' and 'remarkable', expressing surprise that the children combusted at the same time, yet he was prepared to dismiss this as yet another 'shocking coincidence'.

I have seen television documentaries where twins – either identical or otherwise – seem to share some form of bond, almost 'psychic' for want of a better word, and one can sometimes experience mental or physical sensations which the other one is going through. Of course, these girls weren't twins, but it is certainly interesting to note the closeness of their ages, so perhaps a similar bond existed between them.

So the answer could lie here. Or perhaps, if there really is some form of rare medical condition which makes particular people more prone to spontaneous human combustion, then why shouldn't it exist within relatives of very similar age?

The fact that neither had any matches, and there was no evidence of where the flames had come from, makes this case a particularly intriguing example of possble spontaneous human combustion.

However, I do not believe that there is a supernatural or paranormal force at work here and, while I admit there are such things as genuine coincidences, I do not believe that this was one such example.

Two girls, virtually the same age, living in separate houses – not only within view of each other, but also, as you look across the valley, almost exactly opposite each other, virtually in a straight line – who both die from burning at exactly the same time. I believe the answer lies within the apparent coincidences, rather than an otherworldly force, though, unfortunately, I cannot offer a solution.

three

THE BODY
ON THE COAL-PILE

It was 3.45 p.m. Wednesday 11 June 1980. The young man stood rooted to the spot. A man's body was lying on top of a pile of coal, in his father's coal-yard in the town of Todmorden, West Yorkshire. Trevor Parker took a few steps forward and peered up at the body. The man was lying on his back, fists clenched, eyes bulging, staring skyward – and from the expression of horror on his face, he looked as if he had died of fright. A number of small, oval-shaped burn marks were evident on the side of the man's head and neck, which Trevor would not touch.

He later told a journalist:

It [the body] was just lying there plain in sight. I didn't know whether the man was dead or alive, so I called the police and an ambulance. I was very frightened. I didn't want to be out there by myself. The body gave me an eerie feeling. I have no idea how the man got in the yard, but I know one thing for absolutely certain – there was no body on that coal-pile when I loaded my truck earlier in the day.

It was not only the fact that he had found the man there at all that was odd, for there was one more point. It would have been a difficult task for any man to climb up the side of the coal-pile, but even more so in this case because it had been drizzling for most of that day and, as it was discovered later, the man would have found climbing almost impossible because of his breathing problems. Finally, the coal-pile had not been disturbed with anything resembling footholes or marks. So how did he get there?

Twenty-five minutes later, two police officers arrived to inspect the body and question Mr Parker. He told them what he knew, but there seemed to be nothing that could throw light on the mystery. The man had no documents on him, so he was to remain unidentified for several days.

Eventually, appeals by police through local newspapers and local radio would identify the body as that of Zigmund Adamski from the West Yorkshire village of Tingley, who had disappeared on his way to the local shops five days previously on Friday 6 June 1980.

The body was transferred to the mortuary at nearby Hebden Bridge, and that night, at 9.15 p.m., a consultant pathologist conducted a post-mortem. From his examination, Dr Alan Edwards estimated that the time of death was between 11.15 a.m. and 1.15 p.m. This was around

Todmorden, where the body was discovered. (Courtesy of Stephen Gee)

NEW RD, HEBDEN BRIDGE

Hebden Bridge, where the post-mortem was carried out. (Courtesy of Stephen Gee)

eight to ten hours prior to the post-mortem. The body, therefore, had been in the yard for at least two-and-a-half hours before its discovery. No major physical injuries were discovered – certainly no internal injuries – which showed that he had probably not died from an assault of any kind. There were, however, the curious oval-shaped burn marks on the left of the neck and also below the left ear. This had caused a slight loss of skin and a brown discolouration. A tacky substance had been applied to them, presumably a form of ointment. According to the newspapers at the time, the 'gel' had been tested and it could not be identified, though exactly how it was tested and by who, I have not been able to discover.

Dr Edwards thought that the marks indicated contact with a corrosive substance but he could not ascertain what it was. Although the burns were not minor injuries, he was sure they were not the cause of death. However, they could have caused some alarm to Adamski and brought on a heart attack. The final verdict was 'natural causes' – as he had obviously died from heart and chest disease.

The site of the former goods yard, near the railway line at Todmorden station, where Mr Adamski was found.

The local shops in Tingely, which Adamski never reached.

Even though he was found minus his shirt (which was never recovered) he had not been sleeping rough. His body showed that he had only day's growth of stubble – so he had evidently been staying somewhere and, even though his stomach was empty, this merely indicated that he had not eaten on the day of his death. Dr Edwards found an abrasion on the man's right thigh, and superficial cuts on both his hands and knees.

Zigmund Jan Adamski was Polish by birth and, like so many of his fellow countrymen, he had settled in England having been forced to flee his country during the war. He set up home in Tingley, became a coal miner and, in 1951, married Leokadia or 'Lottie'. When she became so ill that she was confined to a wheelchair, Zigmund needed to spend more time with her. His own health, too, was under question, and he had been off work for several months; a lung deformity often made breathing difficult – and it was this extra factor that persuaded Zigmund to apply for early retirement. This was initially rejected, but his company's decision was reviewed quite soon after and the application subsequently accepted.

Fielden Square, Todmorden. (Courtesy of Stephen Gee)

Unfortunately, the reversed decision arrived in the post the day after he disappeared. Upsetting though this was, family and friends were sure he had not gone missing through depression. He would never have left his wife; neighbours spoke of how devoted the couple were to each other.

On the day that Adamski disappeared he had been shopping in Wakefield town centre with his cousin and her son who were visiting the Adamskis from Poland. That afternoon, the trio returned to the couple's home and sat down to a fish-and-chip dinner. Adamski was enjoying his cousin's visit and he was also very excited as he was due to give away his god-daughter in two days' time. He had a speech specially prepared for the occasion, and would not have let the couple down for any reason.

At half-past three, Adamski announced that he would pop down to the local shops to buy some potatoes. He grabbed his jacket (containing wallet, driving licence and some small change), and left the house. Passing a few desultory comments with a neighbour washing his car, he set off to the shops – but he never reached them.

When Adamski did not return home that evening, Lottie contacted Wakefield police to report his disappearance, but despite intensive police enquiries and an appeal in local newspapers, their investigations drew a blank – that is, until his body was discovered.

The Calder Valley had long been considered a hotbed for UFO sightings, and it wasn't long before UFOs had caught hold of the public's imagination concerning the mystery death; all it needed was for someone to suggest it and the most exotic explanation soon became the most likely. People argued there were too many points that did not make sense for there to be a mundane explanation. While the UFO-alien abduction theory seems wildly improbable, it is pertinent, I think, to include the reasons why the Adamski death was initially linked to this phenomenon.

During the time that Adamski had been missing, many people in nearby towns, including Todmorden, had reported UFO sightings. In addition, just five months later, one of the two police officers who were called to the coal-yard claimed to have seen a UFO hovering above a road in Todmorden on Friday 28 November (see the chapter Out of this World). Whether this encounter or the UFO sightings had any connection to the Adamski death is not known, but all investigators have been unable to find a conventional solution to the mystery.

There are several other reasons why the death was linked to the UFO phenomenon. Adamski had obviously been somewhere during those five days that he was missing, but no one had reported seeing him, and the way his body re-appeared was very odd. It was found in broad daylight on top of a pile of coal with no easy access, and in the vicinity of a busy railway line. No one had reported seeing anything odd during those hours; any effort to place a body in that particular location would have been a hard and cumbersome task, almost certainly resulting in footmarks or some form of indentation in the coal and immediate vicinity. And it would have been a foolhardy and pointless way for anyone wanting to dispose of a body in the first place. The idea that he had simply been dropped from the sky seemed as likely a theory as any.

We should also consider where and when he went missing. Had Zigmund Adamski disappeared during the hours of darkness it would be quite understandable – many hundreds of people go missing at night – but it was early Friday afternoon in late Spring when Adamski set off on his errand, and so it seems even more astonishing that no one saw him after that point. The fact that he never reached the shops obviously means something happened to him on the way there. But what? Even if the UFO abduction theory was considered as a serious alternative, it would still sound implausible in light of this factor alone. What did they do? Beam him up – and down again – in broad daylight, just like Scotty does in *Star Trek*?

By far the most tenuous link to UFOs concerned the victim's surname. In the 1950s, a Polish-American named George Adamski penned a best-selling book claiming that he had been abducted by aliens. The 'evidence' he produced was cine footage of what purported to be an alien craft moving erratically in front of the camera. Although this was probably a hoax produced by dangling a model from a length of wire, George Adamski, even today, is championed as one of the leading lights in UFO circles – so to speak – and hailed as an 'alien abductee'.

Zigmund Adamski had been described as a loving family man with no known enemies; although dogged by bad health, he had a lot to live for. Here was a man who had been a prisoner of war, escaped the horror of the Nazis, settled and married and worked in England, only to die in the most mysterious of circumstances.

There were several myths built up around the mystery, presumably through a mixture of factors: the constant recounting of the case; the sensationalism of the tabloid press; a number of UFO fanatics who may have bent the truth here and there to make the case for alien intervention and a government cover-up appear more likely; and a number of filmed reconstructions.

These filmed reconstructions got several of the basic facts wrong, including when he disappeared, then reappeared, and what he was wearing on both occasions. However, the biggest discrepancy was how the body was discovered. This version states that at 10 p.m., two coal-yard workers entered the yard seeing nothing unusual; they walked to the rear of the yard checking the piles of coal as they went, and only saw the body on returning to the gate. They said it had not been there on entering. The last point appeared in some filmed reconstructions for documentaries, which included, I have been told, the television series *Strange... But True?*

Admittedly, the UFO connection still seems feasible after taking these discrepancies into account – and the case remains unique in the annals of UFOlogy because the police publicly stated even they had considered UFO abduction as a possible explanation before eventually dismissing it.

Adamski disappeared in broad daylight in a built-up area, then re-appeared in broad daylight in a built-up area. The burn marks were caused by a corrosive substance that could not be identified. The ointment which had been applied to the burns also could not be identified.

No one had reported seeing him during the five days' disappearance. The way his body was found, face up, on top of a coal-pile with no easy access, lent weight to the theory that he had been dropped from above.

The main point, however, was the look of horror on Adamski's face. Despite the myths, that horrified expression was genuine. Everyone who saw and examined the body, including his widow who had to identify him, vouched for that terrified look. She said, 'I still do not know how my husband died. The worry just goes on and on.'

West Yorkshire coroner Mr James Turnbull assured Mrs Adamski that he would leave no stone unturned until he discovered what happened to her husband. He postponed the inquest three times as enquiries were still continuing, hoping that police would procure a new lead in the case, but none were ever forthcoming. He said:

> As a trained lawyer, I have to rely on facts. Unfortunately, we have not been able to uncover any facts that may have contributed to this death. I tend to believe that there may be some simple explanation. However, I do admit that the failure of forensic scientists to identify the corrosive substance which caused Mr Adamski's burns could lend some weight to the UFO theory.
>
> As a coroner, I cannot speculate. But I must admit that if I was walking across Ilkley Moor tomorrow and a UFO came down, I would not be surprised. I might be terrified, but not surprised. I cannot believe that all the thousands of reports of this sort of phenomenon, covering almost every country in the world, and going back through the ages, result from human error.

My enquiry to the Home Office concerning the case, purposefully addressed to no specific department, resulted in a reply from a Mr Butler of the Violent Crimes Unit. Therefore, although Adamski died from a heart attack and there were no signs of physical assault, the Home Office evidently considered a crime had been committed by person or persons unknown.

The village of Tingley where Adamski lived is a combination of old semi-detached homes and new housing estates, which line both sides of a busy dual carriageway, 2 miles from the town of Morley. Admittedly, some of the housing developments have been constructed since 1980, but the village could never have been described as quiet, sleepy and rural, as it has been before, since there appears to have been a busy thoroughfare running through its centre for many years.

In a bid to solve the mystery, I visited the village with my camera to take some location shots, and decided to re-trace his steps. Leaving his house in Thornefield Crescent – a cul-de-sac of semi-detached houses, Adamski talked to the last known person to have seen him alive: a neighbour washing his car, who asked him if he was going for a drink (an odd comment on its own, because some reports state that Adamski was teetotal, and at this time – before the British licensing laws changed – the pubs were closed between 2 p.m. and 5 p.m.).

Leaving his own street, he would have had to cross a small slip road, which now leads to a new housing development. He would have skirted a low stone wall for a few hundred yards, then completed his journey to the shops past a row of semi-detached homes, until reaching a crossroads, where he would be facing the shops directly on the other side and the Bull public house, a few yards to the left of them.

The walk is a distance of around 1 mile and Adamski would have been in full view of the residents' homes on both sides of the road, not to mention the busy rush-hour traffic, particularly at 3.30 p.m., as it was on that Friday afternoon. If he didn't reach the shops, then

Ilkley Moor.
(Courtesy of
Mike Hall)

Thornefield
Crescent,
Tingley.
Zigmund
Adamski began
his fateful
journey from
here.

Mr Adamski's
likely route to
the shops.

something must have happened to him on the way there. Either a car stopped and picked him up – which would suggest a purely random attack – or else he met someone he knew, perhaps a resident of one of the houses on his route or in another part of the village – who asked him in for a chat. Either way, it is amazing in an area heavily populated and busy with traffic that no one remembered seeing Adamski on his way to the shops. The chances of him accepting a lift to the shops would have been unlikely. The traffic on his side of the road was moving in the opposite direction and the remaining distance was minimal and the weather fine.

In April 2001, I appealed for information regarding the case to the readers of a Yorkshire newspaper and I received several replies. One came from the head of a UFO research group who, judging from his letter, had got many facts incorrect. He also stated, as many UFO believers do, that there was a government cover-up. His evidence for this was solely that the police refused to give him any information on the case because the police file was deemed classified.

My own enquiry to the West Yorkshire Police received exactly the same reply. However, all police case files are classified and the chief constable, Detective Chief Superintendent Brian Taylor – who has been of great help to me in my previous writings – simply stated that all information relating to the case had been released to the public and was therefore available from back issues of the local paper. Two enquiries to the *Evening Courier*, in Halifax, over the course of several months, failed to help me, as the file on Zigmund Adamski had gone missing.

The most interesting reply from my newspaper appeal came from Adamski's former driving instructor, who preferred to remain anonymous. He said that the Lofthouse Colliery Disaster in March 1973 claimed the lives of seven miners – only one body was ever recovered – and that Zigmund Adamski personally knew some of the men who had died. And he may certainly have died in the disaster himself, had he not taken the day off to do his driving test with the instructor.

In the absence of any clues pointing to a solution, there is one possibility that should be considered. Of all the articles and books that have discussed and analysed the case, not one of them has ever pointed out a possible connection – even though it has been staring them in the face. A coal miner goes missing for five days and is found dead in a town with which he has no known connection. Of all the places he could have been found, he was discovered on top of a pile of coal in a coal-merchant's yard. Can this 'coal connection' be some bizarre coincidence – or may there be something in it?

Assuming this was a crime and that someone abducted him then dumped his body after he died of a heart attack, then why dump his body in a coal-yard, sandwiched between a busy train station and a residential area?

Wherever Adamski was when he died, it would have made more sense to wait until nightfall, drive his body into the countryside and deposit it there, where he may not have been found for days, weeks or even months, and there would be nothing to link him with anyone or anything. Instead of this, his suspected abductor(s) dumped his body in daylight – taking a huge risk of being seen – in a busy area on a Wednesday afternoon in a populated area. Bearing this point in mind, we must first face the possibility that the body was brought into the coal-yard through the gates. Therefore, how did they know that 1) the coal-yard gates were always left closed but unlocked during the daytime; 2) there was no one present in the yard at the time to witness the dumping of the body?

The only solution is that Adamski must have died very near to the coal-yard or train station. For the same reason that an abductor would not have risked transporting a body into such a busy area during the daytime, then that same abductor would not have risked transferring the

The road to Todmorden railway station.

body from the immediate vicinity to somewhere further away, running the risk of being seen by someone. So they deposited it in the coal-yard, plain for all to see.

And yet the question remains: why carry the body to the top of the coal-pile? It would have taken two people to achieve this – and how did they remove any traces of their footmarks from the side of the heap? But there is another possibility.

Adamski was chased by someone; he hid in the coal-yard, found there was no escape, was cornered and threatened by his attackers, hurried up the coal-pile in a desperate attempt to escape, then promptly dropped dead of a heart attack. If this is the case, however, then why did no one see him being chased? And why did he run into the coal-yard rather than shouting for help and approaching someone at a residential house or at the train station? And what was he doing in Todmorden in the first place?

Having considered the two abduction theories – both terrestrial and extraterrestrial – and found that neither of them adds up, there are, in my view, only two remaining solutions that makes sense.

Perhaps he had a heart attack; it may have been only a mild attack, and he may not even have collapsed or lost consciousness, but it has been known for some victims of heart attacks to lose their memories, albeit temporarily. So, he gets on the next bus and, for whatever reason, winds up in Todmorden.

Alternatively, Adamski visits Todmorden of his own free will. He approaches the coal-yard for whatever reason. While in the vicinity of the coal-yard – perhaps already inside the yard – he suffers a heart attack. He staggers up the coal-pile in a desperate attempt to peer over the fence and call for help, but it is too late. He collapses, falling onto his back, and dies in pain, explaining the expression of horror, bulging eyes and clenched fists, leaving nothing – save an enigma.

But what caused the burn marks? What happened to his shirt? And why was he in Todmorden, 30 miles away from where he lived? The mysterious death of Zigmund Adamski is known the world over, primarily because of its supposed connection to UFOs, but also generally as an unsolved mystery. There are many unanswered questions, and we know too little of the intricacies

▶ ONE MAN'S CRUSADE: Zigmund Jan Adamski's mysterious disappearance more than 20 years ago is now being probed by Writer Andy Owens, right.

Bid to solve riddle of 20 years

Yorkshire Evening Post THURSDAY 19th APRIL 2001

BY ANDREW HUTCHINSON

AN AUTHOR has embarked on a crusade to solve the mystery surrounding the death of a Yorkshire miner more than 20 years ago.

Writer Andy Owens is keen to shed some light on the circumstances leading up to the death of Polish-born Zigmund Jan Adamski in June 1980.

The 56-year-old disappeared from his home in Tingley, near Leeds, on June 6, 1980 and was found dead in the market town of Todmorden five days later with odd oval burn marks on his neck. The back of his head had also been shaved and he had cuts to his hands and knees.

One theory at the time of his death was that the father-of-two had been killed by aliens. An open verdict was recorded at an inquest.

Mr Owens has already featured Mr Adamski's case in his book Yorkshire Stories of the Supernatural in a chapter labelled "unsolved."

But he is now determined to delve deeper to uncover the truth and is looking for the public help to assist in his search for an answer to the mystery.

Mr Owens, 33, from Illingworth, near Halifax, said he was intrigued by the circumstances surrounding Mr Adamski's death.

"It can't be an accident or suicide because of the burn marks," said Mr Owens. "There are no clues to suggest what actually happened to him. It is all very strange."

Mr Owens said the first port of call in his attempt to shed some light on the mystery was to contact police for help. "They told me that the files are not open to the public." The search is now on to trace Mr Adamski's friends and family or anyone whom he may have come across in the months and weeks leading up to his death.

"I know that some of his family went back to Poland following his death but I have no idea whether there are any still living in Yorkshire."

Left and opposite: My search for information regarding Mr Adamski's fate included appeals in the *Yorkshire Evening Post* and *Psychic News.* (Courtesy of the *Yorkshire Evening Post* and *Psychic News*)

of Adamski's life to reach any definite conclusions. If his widow, his family and the police cannot throw any light on his disappearance and death, then how can we expect to do so?

But there is one factor which seems to dismiss the UFO/alien theory. The original press reports from the local paper *Evening Courier* clearly state that as a result of the police's appeal for information, it was found that Adamski was seen drinking in a public house in Todmorden on the morning that he died. The name of the pub is not specified and my interview with local reporter John Greenwood, who looked into the case himself, did not unearth the names of the landlord or any other witnesses, but if it is true, it disproves the theory that the man was abducted – in whatever sense – from Tingley then relocated five days later to Todmorden. This detail has been constantly overlooked by various researchers of the mystery.

We will probably never know what happened in the last five days of Zigmund Adamski's life and yet, by considering the pros and cons of the most popular theories, perhaps we have at least made some progress in highlighting the probable and dismissing the improbable.

Author seeks psychic help to solve alien mystery case

AN author has appealed to mediums to help solve the bizarre mystery of a miner who was found dead in mysterious circumstances over 25 years ago, *writes Tony Ortzen*.

Polish-born Zigmund Adamski, 56, went missing in broad daylight on his way to the shops in the village of Tingley, near Leeds.

"He was found dead five days later, 30 miles away in the town of Todmorden, with which he had no known connection," author Andy Owens told PN last week.

"It obviously wasn't murder as he died of a heart attack. However, his shirt was missing, he had an incision on his right thigh and cuts on his hands and knees."

Mr Adamski's body also suffered "several strange oval-shaped burn marks on the side of his neck and ear. One half of the back of his head had been shaved.

"A substance had been applied to the burns, which scientists failed to identify."

Mr Adamski fled his native Poland during the second world war to escape the Nazis. To colleagues at Lofthouse Colliery, his death was a complete mystery.

Mr Adamski's body was lying on top of a pile of coal. He was

ANDY OWENS: *"In these days of showbusiness, celebrity, money and power, it is a sobering thought that the Spiritualists I have met with work without charge."*

wearing a suit, but his shirt, watch and wallet had vanished.

Even though Mr Adamski had been missing for five days, he only had one day's growth of beard.

James Turnbull, the coroner who dealt with Mr Adamski's death, commented, "The question of where he was before he died and what led to his death just could not be answered."

Exhaustive checks failed to reveal records of Mr Adamski being treated at any hospital during the period he was missing.

One of the most famous UFOlogists of the time – also called Adamski – believed that aliens abducted the Yorkshire miner by mistake.

Speculation of an extraterrestrial encounter was fuelled by

■ *Continued on page 2, col 1*

As a curious postscript to the above, I had a wild and quite eccentric idea to help me solve the mystery. Could a Spiritualist medium contact the late Mr Adamski to ask what happened to him? It was a strange idea, but given the subject matter of this book, I thought it was worth a try.

I contacted Tony Ortzen, long-standing editor *of Psychic News* – the world's only weekly paper for Spiritualists – who kindly offered to do an article about my quest, appealing for help from Spiritualists. I had several offers, one from a self-styled exorcist who rang me at all hours, promising that information would 'come' to me. It didn't. The second came from a medium who spent a long telephone conversation recalling how she had used her 'second sight' to help the police find missing persons, which was very impressive. She also promised to help me – and didn't.

However, several readers of *Psychic News* contacted me with helpful advice on how to go ahead in my investigation. One of the readers suggested I approach a trance medium, as they had been quite helpful in similar situations. And it was then that I recalled how I had interviewed a trance medium for one of my previous books, *Haunted Dorset* (co-written with my friend Chris Ellis), and I contacted him with my rather odd request.

Royston Breeze and his wife Barbara are members of a Spiritualist Church and, by a strange coincidence, Royston had also worked as a miner in West Yorkshire, though he didn't know Zigmund Adamski. When I told him what I wanted, Royston said that they received many such requests and that each one was put forward at their meetings. He explained that the spirit of a Revd Edward Wallace Perkins, described as a former vicar in the south west of England from the mid-nineteenth century, would be consulted. How? As a trance medium, Royston would go into a trance and the reverend would speak through him. Barbara would put to him the various requests, and the whole session would be recorded on a tape player, after which Roy would send the tape to me.

Although the question-and-answer session revealed no new details, or a solution to the mystery, I include it here as an interesting postscript to the above story.

The transcript of the recording goes as follows:

(Revd Perkins speaking through the trance medium Royston Breeze; 12 April 2006)

Revd Perkins: You were going to ask something?

Barbara Breeze: I was going to ask a question on behalf of Royston, I do believe. He had a letter from a gentleman wanting to know how a man had died. Was it in unusual circumstances? That there were marks on the man's neck... healed by a gel that's not even part of this Earth's existence and then we go into the question of whether it was alien abduction or stuff like that.

Do we really need to get into this, trying to find out all of this for this gentleman, or should we just pass it over?

Revd Perkins: Yes. Well the reply would be as you expected, my dear. Often, what another person thinks is contrary to good order and also to the benefit of many, so what they think is entirely in their area, one always needs to question the motive behind perhaps what is openly acceptable, but at another level it's not quite as truthful.

We're trying to be charitable to all concerned. The gentleman that is mentioned, who was referred to. Now, if we may use terminology that you understand – the gentleman died naturally – in that every death is natural and every death is different. But the person died naturally and chose, after a certain amount of reflecting upon his life, to go to, we shall call it, Level Four and there was no reason seeing that he had cleared his last life.

At Level Four, they need to progress in whichever [way] they feel is necessary and good for them. If there is continued thought from the physical or lower vibrations, it will draw them like a magnet, even if they don't want to be. You may say that a person that is held in bad thought is, in spirit, going through their hell, for every step they go forward there is somebody thinking about the steps they have taken in their past, and they may wish to rub out, erase, those bad actions because they truly understand that the only way to move forward is into brighter, lighter realms. And to take the big step between 1,2,3... and 4 – is quite an important decision for them and they will go with advice. Therefore, should it be you ask of us, we would say at our Level it would not be acceptable to bring another back.

But there would be, there would be, certainly of those recently departed (whom have) not, as it were, taken up the full education available, and they would help them with all the details. It is not for you, at that level.

We don't wish to tell you. We wish you to make your own mind up, but we have to expand somewhat and say, 'Do you feel it is correct to bring to this person, this dear soul, who wishes and desires, and has a will, to move forward, to remind us of that which they wish to leave behind?'

And the other consideration is for what purpose would there be for that person's life to be revealed? Well, we have told you it was a natural death, so is it to be that this author, as a part of his profession of selling, or trying to sell, stories to be published, more important than the wishes of the dearly departed?

Barbara: No, definitely not.

Revd Perkins: Yes. You see, if you were to give another story to the gentleman of another person, then he would be equally happy. If it's given to you to give, then there will be a reason or a purpose behind it. You would have the appropriate witnesses at other levels to give you details. If you haven't been given that, then it will be but to give some instruction to the person, the author, a little of your knowledge, to say how ill-founded is the solution that he wishes to apply to a 'mystery' as he calls it.

Barbara: Yes, and I do believe that if the author was as well educated in his spiritual beliefs then he would have come to that truth himself without having to ask anyone to do that. Yes, I understand.

Revd Perkins: That's why indeed we have just said that to bring it to his notice if you must communicate it with him, an acknowledgement at least would be sufficient, and if you do bring it, then you explain that he died of natural causes to your certain knowledge, which we are telling you, and the teachings you may apply in your own way to say that he has moved forward and has no further desire to communication, whether it's to prompt the solving of a mystery or whether it is to make this author the richest man in the world!

Barbara: Thank you very much. That is very well put and understood. Thank you.

Revd Perkins: I do hope we are not being too unkind to the author. It's like all authors, that they can only work with material that comes their way.

Barbara: It's his experience he's going through.

Revd Perkins: That is why it is much better to be inspired – like yourself.

(Pause)

Barbara: I'm enjoying listening to the dawn chorus. The birds are beautiful.

Revd Perkins: Well again, the delight of doing that which is natural. And those that study the animal world will give reasons – in human terms – why creatures do this or the other. They will say 'They sing because of territorial rights'. They sing because it's the most natural thing for them to do.

The flowers grow because they need to improve on what they were, to what they take absolutely for granted, that they will grow into something that is beautiful.

Should it be that there's hindrance in the plan, then they will not lament or cry, but they will try to alter the conditions as best they can. They will grow stronger seed or make sure that they are liberated in alternative soils, or whatever it is (that) it is natural that they'll do.

Barbara: Royston has set some sunflower seeds and I know he is looking forward to watching them grow.

Revd Perkins: Yes.

Barbara: Yes.

Revd Perkins: But again, Royston will need to obey the natural law. And the natural law will not be pushing the seeds in the ground. They will find their way into the ground, but the intention is good and the cultivation is good for the flowers and for Royston.

(End of recording)

four

BEWARE - BIG CAT!

Barbara Alexander was amazed by what she saw at 5.30 a.m. on Friday 30 April 2004. In fact, she was so amazed she made a note of the exact time and date in her diary.

> I looked out of the window of our kitchen and saw a large black cat, with a long, thick, curving tail trotting along on the far side of the road next to the grass verge. It was very much bigger than a domestic cat and moved in more of a 'loping' way. I ran outside, but by the time I got there it was gone. I have not seen it again. I described it to my husband and we looked up some pictures and thought it may be a puma or something like that.
>
> In May 2005, a map was printed in the *Huddersfield Examiner* with cat sightings marked on it, indicating that these big cats have been seen around this area, which I had not been aware of at the time of my sighting, since we had only moved to our village, near Holmfirth, a month before my sighting.

Big cats have been reported from many country villages around West Yorkshire since the beginning of the century, and the first area to have reported sightings was Denby Dale, near Huddersfield, in the year 2000. That summer, police received many calls from people in the Denby Dale area. This big cat was thought to be black in colour and the sightings had coincided with a number of lambs being killed.

John Radley, a postman of Denby Dale, said, 'It looked like a long black cat but not as big as a puma.' Farmers have said they have found claw marks on the animals which they have lost to the mystery predator.

Heather Holmes, RSPCA spokeswoman for West Yorkshire, said she urged anyone who had a sighting of a wild cat to telephone them with a detailed description of the animal and the circumstances of the sighting. 'Eight times out of ten, from the description, we know it is not a wild animal,' Ms Holmes said. 'There are some big cats in the wild who are descended from animals who were let loose after the Dangerous Wild Animals Act came in. Some people who did not wish to apply for a licence set them free.'

A cat, the size of an Alsatian, was spotted in remote fields near Hade Edge. The witnesses describe it as 'a muscular feline, with a swishing tail, stalking through a field.' A farmer of Greenfield, near Saddleworth, saw a large creature with orange eyes, which he shot at. He thought he may have hit it, but found no sign of a carcass.

No known footage of big cats exist in West Yorkshire, but this was taken just over the border in Derbyshire, by Phillip Grey. More stills from this footage can be found at www.bigcatmonitors.co.uk. (Courtesy of Philip Grey)

In April 2002, it was reported in the *Huddersfield Examiner* that Stanley Shaw, a farmer at Kirkburton, went searching for a missing lamb and found it savaged – with its head missing. He said:

> Its head, neck, and innards and part of the ribs had all gone. It had been dragged by something from one end of the field to the other. But there was no blood on the parts that were left. It couldn't be a fox and I don't believe it was a badger. I've never had trouble with badgers. The way it's been eaten seems wrong. Whatever did it, it's a very clean eater.

He thinks that a fox or dog would have made more mess – and eaten only a small amount of flesh. He told the newspaper, 'I am mystified and I'm worried about the other lambs. I don't know what to do for the best.'

There were intermittent sightings of big cats throughout the county from as far afield as Ravensthorpe, Dewsbury, Cleckheaton, Mirfield and the Spen Valley. In Cleckheaton, Debbie and Stuart Ross and their daughter were walking their three rottweillers in the large field behind Whitcliffe Mount School. Mrs Ross described what happened next:

> My husband told us to stand still. The animal was as big as one of our dogs. It was pure black with shiny eyes, its ears were very pointed and its tail was huge. It was much bigger than an ordinary cat – a hell of a lot bigger – and was just sitting on the path we were on. We got to within about 50m of it, when it casually walked off into some bushes, after which Stuart heard it growling.

In Mirfield, a man (who didn't want to be named) was out shooting one night and later told how he saw the beast near the town's railway station. He said:

Above: Park Road, Elland. A big cat has been sighted on this road. (Courtesy of Stephen Gee)

Right: Westgate, Elland. (Courtesy of Stephen Gee)

As I shone my light I saw a rabbit and a dark shadow. I walked off but heard it following me and growling. I was within 10 to 15yds of it. I had no doubt it was a big cat. It was black, muscular with a very wide head; certainly not a domestic cat. I had never seen anything like this and I was very scared. I was ten minutes from my car and alone.

Rosealene Allan told how she and her husband were walking across a bridge on which crosses Spen Beck, heading towards the Spenborough sewage treatment works:

What we saw was black and it padded across the footpath and went under a gap in the fence. It left a print which was much too big for a domestic animal. Our dog stood still and the hairs on her

Shibden Valley, Halifax, the scene of livestock killings by a mystery predator.

Cunnery Wood. Could this be the lair of one of the West Yorkshire big cats?

back stood on end. Our dog would have approached another dog and chased a moggie. Since then my husband has found what looked to be a young badger chewed and stripped to the bone in the same area.

Then in the same year, there were many sightings in the Calderdale district, and more attacks on farm livestock too. The police received several sightings from local residents from many parts of the area. Calderdale's countryside officer, Edward Ashman, said he received a report of a sighting in the village of Booth, near Halifax. A sighting also came in February from someone walking at Cragg Vale, near Hebden Bridge, and a third sighting came from Park Road, Elland, in July. In August, two sightings of a beast with yellow eyes came from Cunnery Wood, off Shibden Hall Road, Hipperholme, Halifax. Mr Ashman said:

> We have had a number of sightings around Halifax. I've never seen one myself and I haven't seen any deer carcasses, which I would expect to find. But there could be a big cat living around here. People do buy wild animals, realise they can't handle them and then release them into the countryside. Big cats naturally cover a large geographical area, so it's possible it could be the same animal seen in different parts of Calderdale.

Farmers Geoffrey Horrocks-Taylor and Jenny Lawton, who own a flock of sheep near Halifax, found one of their ewes savaged, with all its flesh stripped from its back legs.

Mr Horrocks-Taylor had gone to check his sheep one night. He told the *Evening Courier*:

> They were all OK. Then we went out again at eight-thirty the next morning, (and) we knew something was up. The magpies and crows were all there, but they could not have eaten that much. The whole rear right leg had been eaten away. It went right to the bone. It was horrible. We couldn't understand how it had happened. One dog couldn't have done that. Two dogs couldn't have done that.

When he saw the report of sightings in the *Courier* he began to wonder, and agrees the attack by a big cat would have made sense:

> We live in Shibden and two of the sightings have been at Cunnery Woods which is only four hundred yards from us. I think it is possible it might be something like a big cat that killed our sheep.

His neighbour Jenny Lawton said, 'We have had dogs go for sheep, but they normally go for the throat. Both the sheep's back legs had been completely pulled out. I have never known anything like it.'

A month previously, Bradford man Anthony Thornton was walking his dog, Buster, a cross between a boxer and a Staffordshire bull terrier, in the cemetery in Thornton, near Bradford. Mr Smith told the *Courier*:

> It was weird. I heard a rustling in the bushes and seconds later, Buster came running out with blood spurting everywhere. He had two puncture marks, as if caused by incisor teeth, on top of his head and another two under his chin. I didn't hear any noise when it happened because I think whatever got him must have grabbed his entire head in its mouth.

The dog was covered in cuts and had a chunk of flesh ripped from his right shoulder. Mr Smith is a documentary maker, and he took a pair of night-vision goggles to the cemetery to watch for the beast. He said, 'I definitely saw something on the ridge in the cemetery. It had high, pointy ears and different coloured markings. It looked more like a lynx than a panther.'

Paul Westwood, of Pontefract, said that most of the sightings in West Yorkshire have come from around Halifax and Huddersfield. He said:

> Over the years, I've had quite a few reports from members of the public and wildlife police officers
> of big cats roaming the countryside around this area. Drivers have reported seeing a black panther
> with yellow eyes staring into the headlights of the car.
>
> Others have come from people walking in the countryside. In most cases, the description is of a big
> black cat. Other sightings (in 2007) have been reported in Huddersfield, Ilkley, Wetherby and Dewsbury.

Paul is neither a naturalist nor zoologist. He is simply a man following an interest, and his passion for the subject has led onto greater things. He became intrigued by the big cat mystery back in the seventies, on reading masses of press reports from around the UK on the sightings and investigations into the phenomenon. Inevitably, the press labelled the big cats with intriguing and fearsome titles such as the Surrey Puma, Fen Tiger, Beast of Bodmin and, possibly the most notorious of them all, the Beast of Exmoor. Back in 1983, a squad of snipers from the Royal Marines stalked the countryside in search of this elusive creature, which had savaged as many as 100 lambs and sheep. They hid in undergrowth, rifles at the ready, and waited, and waited, and waited. One night, the quick and agile 'beast' killed a lamb under their very noses, but these skilled and highly professional marksmen left the area after the allotted time period without having fired a single shot.

Paul's interest in the mystery led to him to setting up his own website – Big Cat Monitors – and he receives an average of three reports a week, many of which he dutifully checks out. In fact, he works as a volunteer for North Yorkshire Police, who pass on details of sightings to Paul, and he subsequently interviews the witnesses, to try to ascertain what they have seen. But Paul is cautious. He says:

> Many people are genuinely mistaken about what they have witnessed. Sometimes they see dogs.
> At other times it's feral cats. These are domestic cats which have been living in the wild for some
> time. And, of course, there are feral dogs, too.
>
> There are also optical illusions to consider. The most commonly reported descriptions are seeing
> a black animal, but black objects seen at a distance look larger than they actually are, and domestic
> cats of any colour – even in broad daylight – can also appear much larger.

While a healthy degree of scepticism enables him to sort between real sightings of big cats and honest mistakes, Paul Westwood is not dismissive of all the reports. 'There have been too many sightings of the same type of cat for me to doubt they are out there.'

But if these big cats are really out there, what do they feed on? Leopards tend to go for animals of their own size, such as sheep or goats. Considered *en masse*, there are very few reported attacks on agricultural livestock. The woodlands of Britain are teeming with wildlife such as rabbits and birds, plus larger animals like foxes. Says Paul:

The logo of Big Cat Monitors.
(Courtesy of Paul Westwood)

Rabbits would certainly be part of the big cat's diet. Particularly a big cat like a leopard, with cubs, who would go out hunting prey, then bring it back for her young. And a female leopard with cubs to support will hunt and eat rabbits.

For the most part, Paul's self-appointed task may largely be legwork, travelling the length and breadth of the county, interviewing eyewitnesses and reporting his findings, but he has set off camping in the wilds of both West and North Yorkshire for some first-hand investigation in the hope of spotting one of the animals (though so far without success).

There was, however, one particular experience which he will not forget in a hurry. Paul's closest encounter with what could have been a big cat occurred after he received a call from North Yorkshire Police, who in turn had received a call from two men who had been out hunting rabbits, or 'rabbiting'. They had been within two metres of what they were sure was a big cat and were absolutely terrified. Paul met up with the men, along with a police officer friend, and they went to the location of the sighting.

As they left, the two cars drove back down the track from whence they had come. The two men who had originally seen the creature watched as a large animal bounded in front of their 4x4 and disappeared into the adjoining field.

Paul, the police officer and one of the men jumped from their cars and followed it into the field. But the fourth man – the only one of them who had a shotgun and who had a licence to use it – stayed in the car.

When they reached the field they saw a large powerful animal standing ahead of them, silently watching. Paul couldn't say for definite it was a big cat, but the other two were convinced. Whatever it was, it had big, round, unblinking, yellow-orange eyes. Said Paul:

It remained calm and silent, observing us. It was not in the least bit fazed that we were looking at it. We needed to get closer, but could not do so as there was a dyke between us, so all we could do is shine the torches at the creature. At one point, the torch-light picked out another figure a few metres to its side. It looked like a fox, certainly a lot smaller than the first creature, and was unaware of our presence at the beginning. As soon as it saw us, though, it ran off, but the original shape just sat there, looking at us. I used my night-vision goggles to try for a clearer view but I just couldn't make out the exact shape of the animal in the pitch dark. It was the strangest thing I have ever experienced.

He said that many sightings had been near railways, both used and disused, which is the sort of territory that big cats use.

Big cats in other countries are known to walk along train lines, and often use them as boundary markers. These are rural and quiet and the animals use them to get from place to place without being seen or disturbed. They often hide out in woods, then climb trees, so that they can observe any prey that happens to pass by. Other places they will hide out during the daytime would be old mines and tunnels, caves, old barns and other unused outbuildings. They can be very dangerous and my advice is to stay still. Do not look at the cat in the face as they will see this as a challenge and may attack.

But if there is one thing that puzzles Paul, it is a distinct lack of evidence.

My website includes a series of photographs of what certainly looks like a big cat, walking along a country wall in Derbyshire. A zoologist friend of mine, whose opinions are quoted on the website, and who has always been largely sceptical of big cat sightings in the UK, was convinced that the animal was much larger than a normal-sized feline. Another, rather disturbing, photograph of a dead sheep, is also available to view.

This is the one that made him more open-minded about the possibility of big cats in Britain. He said that the only sort of creature that could have killed a sheep in this fashion was either a big cat or a wolf.

Many of the livestock carcasses I examine have certainly been victims of dogs. Dogs rip and tear at an animal, particularly the throat, but occasionally there are victims with two puncture marks on the back of their necks.

Small prey are killed by a bite to the back of the neck where the canines dislocate the spine. Large prey are killed by a throat bite which blocks the windpipe leading to suffocation. A bite to the back of the neck would be ineffective against large prey since the canines would not be long enough and the jaw not wide enough.

Paul Westwood's website, which has been running since 2003, now receives around 30,000 visitors a year and has had a total of over 100,000 hits. If you have a sighting of what you believe to be a big cat or, better still, photographic or video footage, please contact Paul via his website, www.bigcatmonitors.co.uk.

five

THE COTTINGLEY FAIRIES

In the summer of 1919, Polly Wright went to a meeting of the Theosophical Society in Bradford. She lived in the village of Cottingley, a few miles away, with her daughter Elsie and her husband Arthur, one of this country's first qualified electrical engineers.

Polly was interested in the occult and had had strange experiences such as the recollection of past lives and astral projection. That night, she was there to hear a lecture on 'fairy life' and just happened to tell the person sitting next to her that her daughter Elsie and niece Frances Griffiths had taken photographs of fairies near their home. In early 1920, the leading member of the society, Edward Gardner, examined the prints and then contacted his colleague, Sir Arthur Conan Doyle.

In July 1917, Elsie Wright had borrowed her father's camera and taken two photographs at Cottingley Beck, behind their house. When Mr Wright developed the pictures, and saw fairies caught on film, he considered them to be fake and, after he saw the second picture, banned the girl from using the camera again. However, Elsie's mother Polly was convinced they were genuine. The first shows Frances gazing at the camera as a group of fairies dance on the branches in the foreground; the second, taken that September, shows Elsie with a 'gnome'.

Sir Arthur Conan Doyle wrote the *Sherlock Holmes* stories, which became so famous that the fictional detective is now more famous than his creator. Unlike his character though, Conan Doyle fervently believed in the supernatural, including fairies and other elementals, and was a strong supporter of Spiritualism.

In June 1920, he had been commissioned to write an article about fairies for the Christmas issue of the *Strand Magazine*, and when he heard of the photographs, he contacted Gardner and borrowed copies of them. The title was 'Fairies Photographed – an Epoch-making Event', and the two photographs were used to illustrate the piece, but with the girls' true identities masked by the aliases 'Alice' (Elsie) and 'Iris' (Frances). That issue of the *Strand* was published at the end of November 1920, and the magazine sold out within a few days.

Conan Doyle showed them to Sir Oliver Lodge, one of the founder members of the SPR (Society for Psychical Research). Lodge considered them to be fakes, though bizarrely, he suggested that they were not cut-out drawings, but '…a troupe of dancers masquerading as fairies.'

The Kodak laboratories were cautious, explaining that there were many different ways to fake photographs. Other photographic experts, however, seemed convinced they could be genuine. More copies were made and then distributed widely for further examination. The reaction to the article and photographs was huge, particularly from the sceptics.

Major Hall-Edwards wrote, 'as a medical man, I believe that (putting) such absurd ideas into the minds of children will result in later life in manifestations and nervous disorders and mental disturbances…'

And the magazine *Truth* declared, 'For the true explanation of these fairy photographs what is wanted is not a knowledge of occult phenomena but a knowledge of children.' However, not everyone poured scorn on the photographs. One of Conan Doyle's fellow writers stated, 'Look at Alice's face. Look at Iris's face. There is an extraordinary thing called TRUTH which has 10 million faces and forms – it is God's currency and the cleverest coiner or forger can't imitate it…'

Newspaper reporters were sent to meet the family and interview the girls and, perhaps inevitably, one of the papers dispensed with the pseudonyms and so Elsie and Frances became synonymous with the photographs and were thrust into the limelight for virtually the rest of their lives.

At Conan Doyle's request, Gardner travelled to Cottingley to meet Elsie, Arthur and Polly Wright, together with Frances Griffiths, and he reported that they seemed an 'honest family and totally respectable.'

Buoyed by this report, Conan Doyle suggested a plan: Gardener would supply the girls with two cameras, together with twenty-four photographic plates (all secretly marked so that they couldn't be switched) and then ask them to take more photographs. But the theory behind the plan made little sense. In a rather odd twist of logic, Gardner and Conan Doyle agreed that if the girls could produce similar photographs, then it could be proved that the fairies were genuine. How and why was never ascertained, since if the original photographs were faked, then surely the subsequent photographs would be faked too.

By this time, in August 1920, Frances Griffiths had moved to Scarborough with her parents, but she was invited to return to Cottingley for a few days to stay with the Wrights, and he went to visit them again.

Many years later, Gardner would describe his meeting with the girls in his book *Fairies: A Book of Real Fairies* (1945):

> I went off, too, to Cottingley again, taking the two cameras and plates from London, and met the family and explained to the two girls the simple working of the cameras, giving one each to keep. The cameras were loaded, and my final advice was that they need go up to the glen only on fine days as they had been accustomed to do before and 'tice' the fairies, as they called their way of attracting them, and see what they could get. I suggested only the most obvious and easy precautions about lighting and distance, for I knew it was essential they should feel free and unhampered and have no burden of responsibility. If nothing came of it at all, I told them, they were not to mind a bit.

Polly Wright later wrote to him about the events of the 19 and 21 August 1920:

> The morning was dull and misty so they did not take any photographs until after dinner when the mist had cleared away and it was sunny. I went to my sister's for tea and left them to it. When I got back they had only managed two with fairies. I was disappointed. They went up again on Saturday

afternoon and took several photographs but there was only one with anything on and it's a queer one, we can't make it out. Elsie put the plates in this time and Arthur developed them next day.

PS: She did not take one flying after all.

It is fascinating to look at the reaction of Elsie's parents to the girls' claims of photographing fairies. Elsie's mother Polly, as illustrated above in her letter to Gardner, and as a member of the Theosophy Society, was a believer in 'nature spirits', as she termed them, and believed her daughter's claims; Elsie's father Arthur, meanwhile, remained utterly sceptical throughout his life. He had always admired the creator of Sherlock Holmes until Conan Doyle publicly admitted he believed in the photographs and in fairies in general. He was at a loss to understand how such an intelligent man could be fooled '...by our Elsie, and her at the bottom of the class!'

However, when the three further photographs were delivered to Gardner he sent telegrams to Conan Doyle (who was in Australia at the time lecturing on Spiritualism). Conan Doyle replied:

My heart was gladdened when out here in far Australia I had your note and the three wonderful pictures which are confirmatory of our published results. When our fairies are admitted, other psychic phenomena will find a more ready acceptance... we have had continued messages at séances for some time that a visible sign was coming through...

Conan Doyle included copies of the new photographs in a second article he wrote for the *Strand Magazine*, and also included them in his new non-fiction book, *The Coming of the Fairies* (1922).

The fifth photograph seemed to show several fairies on a bush and Conan Doyle described them in his book:

Seated on the upper left-hand edge with wing well-displayed is an undraped fairy apparently considering whether it is time to get up. An earlier riser of more mature age is seen on the right possessing abundant hair and wonderful wings. Her slightly denser body can be glimpsed within her fairy dress.

In August 1921, clairvoyant Geoffrey Hodson visited the girls, with the view that if anyone else could see the fairies then it was more likely to be a person with psychic abilities. Despite claiming a sighting himself, the girls admitted many years later that they had humoured the poor man to a quite alarming degree. In fact, as the years passed, Elsie and Frances, who had moved away and attempted to stay out of the limelight, inadvertently kept the mystery alive by continually changing their story: first they admitted faking the photographs, then they retracted the statements, denied making them and claimed they had been genuine all along.

In the magazine *The Unexplained*, they told the journalist and author Joe Cooper the fairies were faked – they were simply paper cut-outs held up by hat-pins. However, in September 1976, Austin Mitchell interviewed them for *Yorkshire Television*, and ended with the question, 'Did you, in any way, fabricate these photographs?' Frances replied, 'Of course not. You tell us how she (Elsie) could do it? Remember, she was sixteen and I was ten. So then, as a child of ten, can you go through life and keep a secret?'

A photograph of Frances 'Alice' Griffiths, taken by her cousin Elsie 'Iris' Wright'. The first picture in the Cottingley Fairies series. (Courtesy of Glenn Hill/ NMeM/ Science & Society Picture Library)

And yet, Elsie's artistic ability had always been there for any investigative journalist worth their salt. From the age of thirteen, she had been a student at Bradford Art College and was considered by many to be an 'extremely gifted and accomplished artist' who painted landscapes and portraits, mainly in watercolour, and had also found work in a photographic lab and in a greeting card factory during the First World War.

In the darkroom, her job was to create composite photographs of deceased soldiers, photographically reunited with their families, and during this time, she worked with plate cameras. And in 1978, it was discovered that some of the fairies in the photographs were found to greatly resemble a drawing in the book *Princess Mary's Gift Book* (1915) by Claude A. Shepperson. And yet, despite all this evidence to show that the girls had faked the photographs, there were still the believers.

Harold Snelling, an expert on fake photographs in the early 1900s, said, 'These dancing figures are not made of paper nor any fabric; they are not painted on a photographic background – but what gets me most is that all these figures have moved during the exposure.' And the author William Riley wrote, 'I have many times come across several people who have seen pixies at certain favoured spots in Upper Airedale and Wharfedale.'

Further 'evidence' came to light that suggested the girls had been telling the truth all along. Many years before, in the week before the end of the First World War, Frances Griffith sent a letter to Johanna Parvin, a friend who lived in Cape Town, South Africa. Dated 9 November 1918, it read:

Dear Joe, (Johanna),

I hope you are quite well. I wrote a letter before, only I lost it or it got mislaid. Do you play with Elsie and Norah Biddle? I am learning French, Geometry, Cookery and Algebra at school now. Dad came home from France the other week after being there ten months, and we all think the war will be over in a few days. We are going to get our flags to hang upstairs in our bedroom. I am sending two photographs, both of me, one of me in a bathing costume in our backyard, the other is me with some fairies up the beck. Elsie took that one. Rosebud is as fat as ever and I have made her some new clothes. How are Teddy and Dolly? Elsie and I are very friendly with the beck fairies.

On the back of the photograph, Frances wrote, 'It is funny I never used to see them in Africa. It must be too hot for them there.'

On 25 November 1922, the postcard was rediscovered and later published in the *Cape Town Argus* as an exclusive link to the Cottingley Fairies story. The headline was 'Cape Town Link in World Controversy'. The article included the lines:

…isn't this the best kind of evidence possible that, two years before Conan Doyle even started this controversy, Frances Griffiths believed implicitly in the existence of fairies: so implicitly indeed as to discuss them with no more surprise or emphasis than she discusses her dad, her dolls, and the war?

But the question remains: who sent this postcard to the *Cape Town Argus*? Was it Ms Parvin, or perhaps even Elsie or Frances, who wanted to present some further 'evidence' to back up their claims?

On 17 February 1983, Elsie wrote to photographic expert Geoffrey Crawley after the latter had devoted a ten-page article to the photographs in an issue of the *British Journal of Photography*. In the letter, she states that the girls had faked the photographs, but decided not to tell anyone. Elsie wrote:

…I was also feeling sad for Conan Doyle. We had also read in the papers of him getting some (jeering?) comments, first about his interest in Spiritualism and now laughter about his belief in our fairies. There was also a cruel cartoon of him in a newspaper chained to a chair with his head in a cloud, and Sherlock Holmes stood beside him… He had recently lost his son in the war and the poor man was probably trying to comfort himself with otherworldly things. So I said to Frances, 'Alright, we won't tell as Conan Doyle and Mr Gardner are the only two we have known of, who have believed in our fairy photographs and they both must be many years older than we are, so we (will wait until) both have died of old age. Then we will tell.

Frances Way (née Griffiths) died in July 1986 and, despite their earlier admission that the photographs were fakes, right up until her death Frances maintained that they really did see fairies in Cottingley Beck and that the fifth photograph was genuine. Elsie Wright died two years later in 1988. And the truth died with her.

six

GHOSTBUSTERS!

In December 2005, Dawn Stead formed the group HYPR (Haunted Yorkshire Psychical Research) to investigate allegedly paranormal phenomena. Says Dawn:

> Since I was a child, I had always enjoyed things like the paranormal. Over the last few years I have read and studied the subject, with a view to becoming an investigator, but I kept talking myself out of it. Why? I thought that all the people who are interested in this sort of thing were slightly unhinged, but, in reality, they are normal folk whom you meet every day of the week. I think more people are interested in this subject than are willing to admit for fear of ridicule. It's only when the subject is mentioned in company, that many of these people will open up and add their own experiences.

Two of the HYPR's most fascinating and revealing investigations in people's homes are featured in my previous book *Haunted Bradford*, in the chapter 'Who Ya' Gonna Call?'

MEDIUMS

It may seem that investigations uncover more phenomena when mediums are present, and I wonder if they are essential to investigating teams – in other words, would an investigation be as successful when a team is comprised of non-psychic investigators, armed only with equipment?

Dawn told me her thoughts on the matter:

> I believe in using different tools when gathering evidence and a medium is basically another piece of equipment at your disposal. You can investigate places without a medium and many teams do just that. There are no rules. It simply depends on the methods and tools which you personally want to use.
>
> We originally used two mediums – one of whom, Tracy, left the group two years ago – and we currently have just one, Graham, who happens to be useful in two capacities: firstly as a psychic, and secondly as a psychological nurse/counsellor (his day job). The field of paranormal investigation is

littered with obstacles and you have to pick through these as best you can. Not everyone we meet is of sound mind and body, and Graham proves doubly useful to the team using his expertise in psychology. He needs to give his professional opinion on the people who live/work in the property before I will allow an investigation to take place.

DIFFERENT METHODS OF INVESTIGATION:

Dawn continues:

Divination techniques (dowsing, Ouija board, crystal balls, tarot cards) are sometimes used to try to communicate with the spirit/entity/ghost.

We tend to use several scientific methods but, on occasion, we will use a pendulum or dowsing rods when investigating a haunting. We try to get several different readings besides just the results we get with divination. Unfortunately, divination methods are not measurable in scientific terms, because it cannot be proved exactly what is moving the pendulum or dowsing rod (is it a spirit or psychic energy, or simply the person holding the instrument?), so I think it's important to use several methods together, rather than just relying on one. We openly encourage all our members to use lots of different equipment during our investigations. It's important that everyone knows how to use each item of our personal kit properly, whether it's the laser thermometer, dowsing rods, or whatever.

At the beginning of reports on the HYPR website, Dawn lists various scientific observations and measurements, such as:

Solar Rays: Active
Geomagnetic Field: Quiet
Current Moon Phase: 99 per cent Waning Gibbous
Humidity: 55 per cent

Dawn explains the significance of these:

Without getting into very complex explanations, some of those conditions mentioned cause electromagnetic fields and it is mooted in some circles that high readings of all these states could help ghosts/spirits to manifest themselves. Some think that ghosts need the presence of electricity to appear, and so we use an EMF (electro-magnetic fields) Detector, so if you have high readings at a location, then that could explain more about why paranormal events may occur.

EARTHLY ENERGY

Dawn continues:

EMF meters measure electro-magnetic energy. All electrical items give off electro-magnetic energy from very low levels to very high levels. The readings from these appliances need to be taken into consideration on an investigation. They have to be ruled out as a cause for the haunting. If somewhere has high levels of EMF, there may be lots of electrical equipment, which can make some people feel like someone is watching them, and could also be possibly harmful to their health, if they are exposed to these high levels for long periods of time.

However, it is also theorised that ghosts need energy in order to appear to people. Therefore they supposedly give off this field of energy, and it is this we are trying to measure with our EMF meters.

Also possibly connected to energy is the theory that ghosts draw physical energy from the living in order to appear, or for other methods of contacting us, like moving physical objects, etc. It has been noted on our investigations that camera batteries will drain very quickly, even though they have been fully charged prior to the investigation. Also, some team members will feel physically drained on location, and tire very quickly. One theory to account for this is that spirits will drain a person of their energy, using the person's energy as its own, rather like a battery.

SPOOKY SCIENCE:

Sometimes, mediums will say they are communicating on a one-to-one basis with a spirit, but at other times they will be sensing something called 'residual energy', and I asked Dawn to explain this.

Residual energy is allegedly a haunting based on the 'tape recording' effect, where the 'ghost' is like a past event playing back like a tape recording. The vast majority of reports are made up of this type of case. This is not what we call an 'intelligent haunt'. It's not aware of you, and can neither acknowledge nor interact with the witness: it simply runs through its routine every so often, whether that is walking down a corridor, standing by a window, etc.

Dawn says that it is not yet clear what causes this type of haunting. Could the solution, I ask, lie in the midst of a recognised science such as metereology or geology?

Dawn replies:

It is thought that certain weather conditions may cause some sort of 'playback effect', from the location, such as the fabric of the building. Some areas with large concentrations of rock formations such as limestone and granite allegedly have higher numbers of paranormal activity than areas which don't have these geological components.

EQUIPMENT

The HYPR investigators use many different types of equipment: some hi-tech, and some very basic. Dawn Stead explains:

Infra-red camera helps us to see things in complete darkness. The laser thermometer helps you to keep a check on temperature levels, fluctuations, etc. If someone says that a room feels like it's gone colder, then the thermometer helps us to confirm this, or not, as the case may be.

While HYPR use some sophisticated electronic equipment, they also use basic tools, such as a thermometer (for noting sudden temperature drops) and 'trigger' objects (which are left in locked rooms and circled in chalk, to see if they have moved position by the end of the vigil).

Although this is specialist equipment, Dawn always backs this up with a common garden thermometer, '…in case your laser thermometer starts giving crazy readings, which can sometimes happen!'

She says:

There are theories aplenty in this field [ghost hunting], but at this time, that is all they are: just theories. There is no hard evidence either way, as yet. At the present time, it is only a theory that ghosts/spirits may cause a reading on a gadget such as an EMF Detector. We also use compasses as they are also thought to react to paranormal activity. I always say that you have to experience things for yourself. We are not here to confirm or deny anything. We are here simply to present the evidence and let people make up their own minds about the reality of ghosts and what caused them. I can't prove that ghosts exist. But I can't prove that they don't either!

INVESTIGATION

Amongst the more prominent locations investigated by HYPR was the Red Lion public house at Market Place, in Pontefract.

Dawn recalls the event:

Initially, when I contacted them, I literally rang every pub in Pontefract to see if any of them were experiencing unexplained phenomena. Like lots of other groups who are just starting out,

Left and above: Despite the abundance of haunted castles and stately homes, semis and terraces are the stock-in-trade of the Haunted Yorkshire team.

we wanted to get some investigations under our belt and that involved picking up the telephone to propose investigations. Although we started out investigating pubs and inns, we now mainly concentrate on private residences.

There are several reasons we now avoid pub investigations. The vagaries of investigating pubs can be immense and there are lots of variables to consider before embarking on investigations, such as: how noisy is it going to be? Is it located in the city centre? Are there nightclubs nearby? All of these factors can taint sound recordings, so you have to be so careful when selecting locations. You cannot always foresee problems such as this and tend to learn from experience.

RED LION, PONTEFRACT

The first investigation carried out at the Red Lion by HYPR occurred on 26 February 2005 and the group consisted of eleven people (including Dawn). As the area to be investigated was well away from the bar area, they began while the pub was still open. Dawn recalls what happened next:

By 8 p.m., we had set up our base for the night in an old disused kitchen on the first floor, and the main team set off to explore the rest of the building. When we realised how large the building actually was, we decided we would return at a later date to cover the other floors we did not cover the first time around. This investigation would only cover seven or eight of the rooms.

The first we entered was the old ballroom, and here we took several location photographs, most of which had some form of 'orb' on them. There is much speculation about what 'orbs' are, together with some pretty wild theories. Most 'orbs' can be explained as dust, insects, light refraction, moisture, etc. Unless a photograph was analysed by experts, I would not put my hand on my heart and say that orbs are anything other than what I have listed above.

Our team mediums, Graham and Tracy, both commented on seeing 'people in spirit' dancing around the ballroom and also standing in one corner of the room near a window. We entered a second room and took photographs, but nothing in particular was reported from there.

Then we entered a third room, which we all remembered as the 'infamous room' which had felt tremendously cold when we looked around the building a few weeks previously. More or less straight away, everyone commented on how cold it was! I got out my laser temperature gun, and we all witnessed how the temperature in the room began to drop like a stone! It went from being 2 to 3 °C to minus ten at one point. The temperature outside on the previous night had been above freezing level – 4 to 5 °C – so we were at a loss to explain this massive temperature drop within the room. On several occasions, Tracy would get me to point the temperature gun in a certain area, just as the temperature would begin to plummet.

Then Tracy became aware of a little girl who was singing nursery rhymes as she played there. There was also a wardrobe in the room, which no one seemed to have good feelings about. When we opened the door, the cold literally hit us, as if we had just opened the door of a fridge! Again, there was a sudden temperature drop, and very soon the laser gun measured minus nine inside the wardrobe. Graham felt that someone had been locked in the wardrobe, and whoever it was liked the door to be left open.

We entered several of the disused bedrooms and had varying feelings: some felt fine and some a little uneasy. A couple of the rooms had a certain coldness to them, but not in the same way the other room had! On about two occasions, the EMF meter registered a reading, though the only source of electricity in the room was the wall-fitting near the sink and the ceiling light – but they could not have been responsible for these readings, since neither had any power connected to them! Interestingly, as I was registering these readings, team member Russ took a photograph with a digital camera and on the photograph was a light anomaly in the exact area where I had just taken my readings.

We left the room, closed the door and stood on the landing in total darkness and then we heard the floorboards creaking in the room we had just left, even though there was no one inside.

Into another room, and Graham sensed the presence of a gentleman of the clergy who was seemingly pacing up and down the corridor in an angry fashion. Graham sensed that this man of the cloth had been excommunicated from the church for helping and/or performing abortions.

Soon after, Russ called out that the camera had just switched itself off, which usually indicated a flat battery. However, on switching it back on, he discovered that this was not the case, as the battery power was showing it had four hours of power left! Russ and the rest of the team are still at a loss to explain how this might happen.

The team drew the investigation to a close, but since it had proved to be most eventful, they arranged a return visit for 9 April 2006.

THE SECOND INVESTIGATION

When the team entered the ballroom, the EMF meter was fluctuating between 1.5mg to 2.5mg even though the electricity was switched off and there was no electrical sources in the room.
Says Dawn:

Graham and Tracy paced around the room for a while and were picking up various feelings there. Tracy commented on having a feeling of a children's party here, whilst Graham was standing in the corner of the ballroom and once again picked up on the energy of a woman. Team member Wendy walked over to the point with her dowsing rods which, strangely, crossed at the exact spot where Graham was standing as he was discussing the presence he was sensing. I checked the EMF meter at the spot and it suddenly sprang into life, shooting up to 3mg for a split-second before returning to 1.5mg. Russ, our camera-operator, reported feeling physically drained. He had stopped filming and was feeling very sick, so he went for a sit down.

Graham used a pendulum to assist him to ask 'yes' and 'no' questions of the mystery lady in the corner of the ballroom. She confirmed she had worked there and was happy to remain. She was under forty years of age when she had passed over, and when Graham asked for a date she indicated it was the 1700s.

In the hallway leading to the ballroom, Graham felt a painful stabbing sensation under his ribs on his right-hand side. Again, we used the dowsing rods in this area, and they crossed again, and the EMF meter showed a sudden increase again, too. As Tracy arrived, she too felt a pain in her side, and said that someone or something was touching her head.

Graham used the pendulum again to conduct another 'yes' and 'no' question session. He sensed that the name Oliver Haywood was prominent, who had passed over at the age of sixty-five. At this point the EMF meter read 4.0mg before reducing again to 1.5mg. Graham sensed that Oliver was wearing glasses, a shirt and waistcoat. He was still feeling the painful stabbing sensation in his side, and another name, 'George', also came through to him. Tracy also reported feeling quite sick at this time. Oliver gave Graham a clear indication that he had stabbed George in an argument over money. He had not intended to kill him, but confirmed he had served time for his crime. Graham asked for a date and 1724 was confirmed. Tracy described a knife with a 4in blade, which resembled a bowie knife. Soon after this, Graham said the energy had gone and the EMF meter was confirming there were no further readings of electro-magnetic sources.

In a private flat on the first floor of the building, Tracy picked up the energy of a slim woman in her twenties, with blonde hair, who was dressed in relatively modern clothes, which she described as 1960s fashion. She was about 5ft 7in in height and the name of Joanna came to mind. Once again, the EMF readings were fluctuating and the dowsing rods crossed in certain areas of the room. On entering another room in the same private flat, Tracy picked up on the energy of a man with a large build who had a heart condition, and Tracy also commented that there was a strange 'buzzing' in the room – not a sound but an atmosphere – and commented how she would feel uneasy if she had to spend much longer in there.

We visited the end bedroom on the top floor where Graham had sensed that abortions had been carried out. There was a very high temperature on the laser gun and, once again, the EMF meter showed a slight reading at the point where Graham indicated that the energy was standing.

In the top-floor corridor, every team member agreed that they sensed it was not a pleasant part of the building. Practically everyone in the team reported feeling nauseous here. Russ, Tracy, Wendy, myself and the barmaid all felt physically sick, so we spent only a brief time in the rooms on this floor before leaving. As on the last investigation, Graham was picking up on the energy of the same clergyman, who wasn't very happy that we were all there. Graham commented that he wouldn't be at all surprised if we didn't get something thrown at us if we stayed there!

Graham felt drawn to the back of the pub, and said he was seeing a horse and cart, which appeared to be delivering something (such as coal) in sacks. He said there were the words 'T.A Howarth' written on the side of the cart.

In the reading room, Tracy picked up on the energy of a man, aged around eighty years old. Wendy said she had felt a presence in that room earlier on, and asked Tracy where she was sensing him. It turned out to be the exact spot where Wendy had sensed something.

And at that point, the investigation drew to a close.

NEW AFFILIATION

Dawn recalls:

HYPR were picked out of several hundred applications received every month to become part of the TAPS (The Atlantic Paranormal Society, based in America), which involves representing the group for the Yorkshire region in the UK. It is a great accolade and every member of HYPR is really pleased to be part of this world-wide group. To be part of a much-respected group such as TAPS is an honour.

PROGRESS

Dawn continues:

Personally, I think that paranormal investigation has moved on, making significant progress, from what we were seeing just a few years back. Groups in general are using better ways to investigate a haunting. They are introducing more scientific methods of investigating hauntings and are now looking for other explainations for what could be happening at a property other than a 'ghost', such as normal explanations for allegedly paranormal phenomena.

In fact, HYPR always seek to explain phenomena in 'normal' rather than 'paranormal' terms, so that they can sort between fact and fiction. And there are many different 'natural' phenomena which can confuse and convince even the most sceptical of witnesses. Dawn offers an example:

Humidity can cause people to feel clammy, which in turn makes you feel colder, which may explain why people say they feel 'cold' in haunted houses, even though the temperature hasn't changed. So that is why it is important to take all these readings when doing investigations. They are all possible causes of reported happenings, and it helps us to identify the cause, distinguishing between normal and paranormal.

EVIDENCE

Dawn continues:

> Groups out there really must try to use as many scientific methods as possible because, unless you do, no 'evidence' you gather will fly with the science people; you have to be able to back up your claims, so the more evidence the better. Times have changed and, along with those changes, things have improved!

CONCLUSIONS

I asked Dawn if her investigations had challenged, or even changed, her previous views of life-after-death and the paranormal.

> Not really. Things happen which we can't explain. We try to witness strange happenings and hopefully one day it will be acknowledged that there is more to life than just 'you are born, you die, and that's it!' Already scientists are studying whether 'consciousness' survives clinical death – but the real question is, 'How long does consciousness last after death?' The fact that they now agree that some form of consciousness survives at all is a good start in itself!
>
> I do think there is something we can't explain. Consider the vast in-depth readings that people like Gordon Smith and Tony Stockwell [mediums] come up with, such as details about loved ones who have passed on. They are far too specific just to be guessing. Where does that information come from? We can only guess, at this moment in time.

And so HYPR continue to investigate alleged hauntings of places and buildings throughout the Yorkshire area. All of their services are free of charge and they conduct these investigations purely for their own interest and with the aim of gathering tangible evidence of hauntings.

Says Dawn, 'we investigate a case, under the provision that we are entitled to give our opinion of what may (or may not) be happening at a haunted location.'

★ Any readers experiencing strange activity in their homes or places of work can contact Dawn Stead and the HYPR at www.hauntedyorkshire.co.uk or www.hauntedyorkshire.com.

seven

OUT OF THIS WORLD!

On the night of 28 November 1980, a police constable was driving along Burnley Road on the edge of the West Yorkshire town of Todmorden. This market town lies on the county boundary, bordering on Lancashire (of which it used to be a part), and the Calder Valley in West Yorkshire. Calderdale has long been considered synonymous with the subject of UFOs, and it is one of the so-called 'window' areas where a large percentage of unusual phenomena has been reported.

Just five months earlier, Polish miner Zigmund Adamski had been found dead in a coal-merchant's yard in the town set deep in the Pennines, and Todmorden formed part of 'UFO Alley' due to the number of UFO sightings which had been reported from this area, in very high frequency when compared to sightings in other parts of the UK.

On the night in question, police constable Alan Godfrey, stationed in the Todmorden area, was on patrol responding to a report that a farmer's cows had gone missing and were apparently wandering through a housing estate in the area.

He patrolled the area for some time but could see no sight of them. He was about to return to base, as his shift was about to end. As he drove back along the road, he became aware of a large object in the road a few hundred yards ahead. His first thought was that it was a bus carrying local factory workers for an early morning shift, which he knew from experience passed this point at around 5 a.m.

However, as he drew nearer to the object, he realised it was not actually on the road, but hovering above it. It was a fuzzy oval shape, rotating at such speed that it was causing bushes at the side of the road to shake. He stopped the car and peered through the windscreen at the object. The constable took out his notebook and began sketching the object. This may sound an odd thing to do in the circumstances, but part of a police officer's role is to keep a notebook on hand at all times, and make sketches of incidents they encounter (such as road accidents).

Suddenly there was a burst of light, and the next thing he remembers, he was driving his car, further along the road, and the UFO had vanished. The policeman turned the car round and returned to the spot where he had seen the UFO. He stopped and got out of the car to examine the part of the road over which the object had hovered. It was dry, though the rest of the road was wet due to the drizzling rain which had been falling for some time.

A Yorkshire UFO? This fairly simple fake, made by the author and his dad many years ago, shows how easily one can be fooled. Although it is only a piece of brown paper stuck on a window, it is as good as many so-called 'classic' flying saucer photographs.

He arrived back at the police station and was surprised to find that it was thirty-five minutes later than he thought it was. What had happened during those missing minutes?

The constable filed a report and, on arriving for his next shift, was asked for a full statement. Later, other reports seemed to tie-in with his own sighting. Another driver 3 miles further along Burnley Road at the same time as the constable reported to Todmorden police station that he had seen 'a brilliant white light', and a police patrol from Halifax had watched 'a brilliant blue-white glow' descending into the Calder Valley towards Todmorden prior to the constable's sighting.

And so the officer filed an official report with his superiors. He was encouraged by the other sightings which seemed to corroborate his own, and the police also offered further encouragement when they decided to release details of his sighting to the press.

The sequence of events in his mind became jumbled in the months that followed and, although what he had been doing during the period of missing time was never resolved, he did experience a vivid image of himself standing outside his car on the road soon after his encounter.

Eight months after his experience, the police officer was filmed undergoing hypnotic regression by MUFORA (the Manchester UFO Research Association) led by highly respected author Jenny Randles, and he subsequently recounted how he had been taken aboard an alien craft and examined by alien beings, though he could not consciously remember any of these details.

Many years later, I attended a UFO evening at the Todmorden Working Men's Club on Burnley Road, organised by Graham Birdsall, the late editor of the now-defunct *UFO Magazine*, and Alan Godfrey once more recounted his sighting back in 1980. From my viewpoint, the constable came across as an ordinary, down-to-earth bloke, with a healthy sense of humour, who was just as bamboozled by his experience then as he had been when it had originally occurred.

In a television documentary on UFOs, Detective Constable Gary Heseltine, a highly trained witness assessment specialist, was interviewed about the website he had created, PRUFOS (Police Reporting UFO Sightings), which included many reports by police officers (including this particular officer). Although Mr Heseltine was not speaking specifically about the constable's

The Fielden Statue, in Todmorden.
(Courtesy of Stephen Gee)

experience, he emphasised that the police are not in the habit of making things up, and only speak publicly if they truly believe that they happened. He explained:

> Police officers do not suffer fools gladly. And if they say they saw something, and they stand up and be counted, they pretty much tell it as it is, because they're used to doing duty reports, they're used to giving statements that illustrate things in a chronological way as if it was presented in court.
>
> The culture of the police officer is this: it's a select club, for want of a better word. But once you're in there, you develop a reputation. You do not stand up and raise your head above the parapet unless you are sincere, because you will absolutely get crucified by your fellow officers if it wasn't true.

The immediate area around Todmorden and the Pennines has long been the centre of much reported UFO activity, and other similar stories – including that reported by Jenny Randles, of a similar 'abduction' of a lorry driver on Burnley Road subsequent to the above encounter – have also been reported in this vicinity.

Stoodly Pike, which stands among the Pennines, looking out over Todmorden – the scene of much reported UFO activity.

CLOSE ENCOUNTERS OF THE AERIAL KIND?

Having read many accounts of possible mid-air collisions or near-misses between UFOs and terrestrial craft I thought that the website of the CAA (Civil Aviation Authority) might contain details of other such cases. Scanning the index, there was a page number relating to an entry on UFOs, and up came a report of a near-miss incident between a passenger jet and an unknown object. What follows is an edited version of the document:

At 06:48 on the night of 6 January 1995, the crew of a Boeing 737 logged a mid-air encounter with an unknown object, whilst flying over the Pennines.

The pilot reported that they were 8 or 9 miles south east of Manchester Airport, flying over some rugged hills when both he and the first officer saw a lighted object flying at high speed in the opposite direction. The first officer instinctively 'ducked' as it went by, so it must have appeared to him to be very close to the aircraft to warrant such action. He recounted how he had seen something in his peripheral vision then followed the object through the glare shield and side window until it went out of sight. He described the object as wedge-shaped with what could have been a black stripe down the side. It made no attempt to deviate from its course and no sound was heard, or wake felt, from the object, despite its apparent close proximity. Both the captain and the first officer were certain that it was solid – not a bird, balloon, kite or meteorological phenomenon.

On investigation, there was found to be no known traffic in the air at that time and vicinity and no subsequent radar contacts were reported. The captain was certain the object had not been a Stealth aircraft – which can also avoid being tracked by radar – which he had seen before and felt he would have recognised.

Following the incident both men independently sketched what they had seen and while they agreed about the shape of the object, they disagreed about the lights. The captain said it had a number of small white lights, rather like a Christmas tree, whereas the first officer felt that the object was illuminated by their own landing lights.

There was a possibility that it may have been a remote-controlled model aircraft, or piloted hang-glider, para-glider or microlight, although each investigating authority felt this was extremely unlikely for a number of reasons: none of these activities take place at night; there are obvious hazards of flying in the dark and these aircrafts are unlit, and there were strong winds on the night in question. Although the possibility of the object being a military or civilian aircraft could not be entirely discounted, it was considered highly unlikely that either one would have been flying at night, without clearance, so close to a busy international airport. The chances of such a flight remaining undetected are slight; the airport is well-served by radars and any movements at those levels would almost certainly have generated a radar response. The microlight theory would have matched the wedge-shaped description, so there remains the possibility that some foolhardy individual was responsible. However, further talks with microlight experts highlighted the extreme improbability. The strong wind, terrain and darkness would have rendered such a flight almost suicidal.

A group of experts analysed the report for the Civil Aviation Authority, saying that despite exhaustive investigations the object remains untraced. Their conclusions state that, 'to speculate about extra-terrestrial activity, fascinating though it may be, is not within the group's remit and must be left to those whose interest lies in that field.' However, an added note states there is no doubt that the pilots saw an object and that it was of sufficient significance to prompt filing a near-miss report. 'Reports such as these are often the object of derision, but the Group hopes that this example will encourage pilots who experience unusual sightings to report them without fear of ridicule.'

eight

BEER AND SPIRITS

THE FORMER GROSVENOR (PUB), IVEGATE, CITY CENTRE

This pub has seen many changes over the years. First it was called The Grosvenor, then it became a Berni's Inn. In December 1984, it was called Bier Kellar. A reporter from the *Telegraph & Argus*, who remains unnamed, recounted his own experience at the inn.

The man recalled how he and his wife went for a drink there on a very hot summer's day, a few years ago, when the Bier Kellar was a newly opened bar. They ordered drinks and were served by the young barmaid. His wife remarked how cold it was in the bar, despite the heat outside. Looking up, the reporter saw a man across the bar polishing glasses, who smiled at him and nodded.

The reporter said to his wife, 'Have another, then if it's too cold here, we'll go,' and approached the bar, whereupon the barman walked out of sight. 'Same again,' he said – but there was no one behind the bar. The man had disappeared. The reporter ran a convenient bell and after several rings, a barmaid appeared. 'Sorry if you were busy, but the barman went off somewhere.'

'Barman! What barman?' she replied. 'There are no barmen working here.'

The reporter described the man as about 5ft 7in, thin, with the short-back-and-sides haircut of the 1930s, with a centre parting brushed back with a Brylcreem gloss. He was wearing a short white waistcoat. By this time, another girl joined the barmaid and both were visibly trembling. One of them said, 'I'm not staying here. There's something spooky about the place,' and they packed up and left. So did the reporter and his wife. They never did get their second drink.

GEORGE AND DRAGON, FLOCKTON

Shortly after the landlord and landlady had moved into the premises in the 1970s, they were sitting in the lounge watching television. It was very cold outside and they had switched on the fire some time before to give it time to warm the room up. As they sat there, the lounge door opened of its own accord and the room went icy cold. The landlord hurriedly searched the building for intruders, without success. As the couple were sitting discussing what had just occurred, the icy sensation vanished and the lounge door opened and closed again as if 'something' had made a brief visit and left. Another search of the building again revealed no one.

The former Grosvenor, in Ivegate, Bradford – haunt of a phantom pint-puller.

The George and Dragon, Flockton, where phantom figures have been glimpsed in the car park.

The Mallard Inn, Ilkley, where staff and customers experienced a sense of being watched.

A man in eighteenth-century clothing has been seen in various parts of the pub, sometimes on the upstairs landing and at other times in an empty room just off the bar.

One guest told the landlord that he had seen two people walk past the open door of the pub, but when he went to investigate, there was no one there. Then it happened a second time. When the customer left, he insisted the landlord see him safely to his car, just in case!

MALLARD INN, ILKLEY

The Mallard Inn, on Church Steet in Ilkley, dates back to 1708 and is haunted by two ghosts. In September 1999, the manager, Chris Bridge, reported that one ghost had been seen upstairs, while the other was said to frequent the bar area itself.

Although descriptions of the non-paying residents have been vague, staff all agree on the sensation of being watched and the feeling of not being quite alone in apparently empty rooms.

Other odd happenings which have been reported including the hand-drier in the gentlemen's toilet switching on by itself and the wine glasses which, bizarrely, have been found on the floor in a triangular formation.

HARE AND HOUNDS, WIBSEY

In February 2000, landlords Louis and Angela Walton moved into this pub with their three children. Over the next three months they experienced a wide range of phenomena including the sound of voices coming from nowhere and doors slamming with nothing to account for it. But the main event, which baffled even the fire service, was the bizarre burning of a porcelain angel figurine.

Louis told Charles Heslett of the *Bradford Star* newspaper:

> We'd laughed off the other incidents, but the fire could have been life threatening. Jason [their son] had gone into an upstairs room to get some cushions for a friend who was staying the night. He just screamed when he saw the flames and ran into our room. Our friend grabbed a wet tea-towel and picked up the angel and put it out.

The leading fire-fighter who attended the fire, Dave Jones, commented that he had never come across anything like this before. He and other officers from Odsal fire station inspected the figurine but remained baffled why porcelain would burn, and why it was the top half of the figure alone which was damaged by the fire. He had spoken to the couple's son and said, 'What I can't understand is that if it had been, say, a discarded cigarette, there would be deeper burns in the wooden mantelpiece and the figure's legs would have been burned – but they're not.'

Louis Walton said:

> A lot of strange things have happened here since we took over. I've been down in the cellars and heard what I thought was [my daughter] calling 'Daddy, daddy,' but when I got upstairs she was playing pool with her sister and had said nothing. Pens, which I use for stocktaking, keep

The Hare and Hound, Wibsey, scene of a mysterious fire and voices from nowhere.

disappearing and re-appearing in the cellar. Bar stools which Angie has put away have been moved out of place and I am even scared to go into the cellar on my own because of the eerie feeling. I'm not one to scare easily, but I think the pub must be haunted.

Some customers sitting in a certain part of the bar have felt sudden chills, described as 'like ice cubes going down their backs,' even though the heating was on full, and dogs wouldn't walk around that side of the bar, as if they had sensed something that the people couldn't.

The journalist also questioned former landlord Martin Devanney, who told how similar things had happened during his four years there. His brother Patrick once saw an old woman walking through the bar late at night:

At first, he thought it was my wife, Janet – but this figure disappeared through the jukebox and into the tap-room. Janet also saw a shape in the corner of the pub when she was cleaning late at night, which scared the living daylights out of her. There were times when going into the cellar just spooked me. You felt you were being watched.

WHITE SWAN, IDLE

The ghost in this 250-year-old pub only makes entrance after dark and wears a long dress with black lace on it and a black veil. There have been at least five independent sightings of an unknown woman, and three other people (including Paul Rowntree, son of landlord Ron Rowntree) have felt her presence.

Ron Rowntree was appealing for local people to come forward with any information about the pub and the haunting. He said, 'We don't know if it's something recent, or whether they go way back.'

One of the regulars was returning to an upstairs disco from the toilet when he saw the woman standing by the dimly lit bar. Mr Rowntree said, 'We could hear his screaming above the music – that's how loud it was. It frightened him so much he was crying.'

The White Swan, Idle, where an unknown woman has been seen standing behind the bar.

The Harp of Erin, Bradford, where a saucy spook bothers the bar maid.

Ron also recalls the time when his son Paul was down in the cellar with a metal bucket:

I just heard the bucket clattering and he (Paul) shot out of the cellar door. I had thirty-two years in the Parachute Regiment and I've seen fear. You can't fake it and Paul isn't the sort to get worried about things, but he was petrified. His eyes were like organ stops and the hair on the back of his neck was standing up. He was so bad I had to slap him to get any sense out of him. He said he hadn't seen anything but had sensed something come out of the wall, and go past him with a whoosh, and the air suddenly turned icy cold.

The Three Nuns Inn, Mirfield, where the discovery of a ram's head led to a multitude of phenomena.

Mr Rowntree said he had never seen the ghost himself, although he had felt a presence. Beer and wine taps on the bar had been turned on when no one was around after closing time.

His wife Joan said:

I haven't seen it, but it moves things. I'll put something down and it will disappear and I won't be able to find it. Then a few weeks later it will be back in exactly the same spot where I left it.

Several customers, and two decorators working in the pub at night, have either seen the ghost or at least sensed her presence. The couple's Staffordshire bull terrier, Taz, has been affected: 'she's a brave little dog but won't go anywhere near the cellar door.'

A customer Tony Parfitt was sitting at the bar one evening when the pub was virtually empty and part-time barman Bob Farndale was standing a few feet away on the opposite side of the bar cashing up.

Mr Parfitt said:

I saw this woman standing next to Bob. She was solid – just like a real person. I asked him who she was and he turned round and said, 'What are you talking about?' I asked him about five times and each time he turned round, she suddenly disappeared, and then re-appeared when his back was turned. It didn't bother me – I wouldn't have minded if I'd been drinking but I hadn't that night.

Mr Farndale turned and looked but didn't see her. 'I kept saying, "What are you going on about? What woman?" I just couldn't see anyone.'

HARP OF ERIN, BRADFORD

When a ghost appeared in the bedroom of landlady Joan Hagyard, she told it in no uncertain terms to clear off. Which it did – but only by turning its attentions to her daughter.

Susan Hagyard told the local paper:

> I can't explain it. But I'll be just pulling a pint at the bar and feel a hand touching my bottom. I keep thinking it must be a customer who's had one too many but when I turn round there's no one else behind the bar. It's eerie.

The pub has a long reputation for being haunted. Pint glasses have shattered, bottles have leaped off shelves, and ornamental plates were hurled ten feet off walls onto the floor. One barmaid suffered a cut head when a glass shattered in her hand for no apparent reason. Susan Hagyard said:

> I blame my mum for telling the ghost where to go. It's all a bit unnerving. It makes my hair stand on end sometimes. But I don't let it worry me. I have more problems with some of the customers on a bad night! I'm sure there must be a logical answer but I haven't thought of it yet.

THREE NUNS INN, COOPER BRIDGE

In the 1980s, building work uncovered a ram's head hidden behind the fireplace in the wall of this hostelry, and so followed a series of strange happenings which are often reported in otherwise peaceful buildings following structural change.

The usual plethora of phenomena occurred – beer taps turning on and off, doors opening and closing apparently of their own free will, together with objects such as plates flying through the air like paranormal trapeze artists!

In his book *Hauntings in Yorkshire*, Steven Wade notes that the landlord told the brewery of the disturbances and they suggested that the ram's head be replaced in the fireplace, after which the phenomena ceased. Steve mentions how journalist Rowland Cooper visited the landlord recently and was told that a guest had insisted he was being watched by a tall grey figure with a beard, though whether this was connected with the psychical phenomena is not known.

TOWER HOUSE HOTEL, HALIFAX

William Thomas and his family experienced several hauntings when they moved into the pub and hotel in the 1970s, though they did not tell guests about them for fear of losing business. A medium visited the family and spoke to the spirits and, after that, very little was reported – that is, until the Thomas family started refurbishing the building and changing the lounge into a bar, which included knocking down walls and sealing off two rooms. From that point, overnight guests complained about the sound of footsteps and banging noises coming from the empty loft.

Mr Thomas saw a young girl who looked about twelve years of age, with long, dark, straight hair, dressed in a white dress or nightie, and another figure, an older woman, presumably the girl's mother; both of them haunted the bedroom belonging to him and his wife. He once saw the woman standing over the bed while his wife was asleep. The woman had her arm raised above her head as if she was about to strike his wife, but when he went to stop her, she vanished.

This is one of many cases of hauntings which have either begun or returned after the internal structure of a building has been changed.

ROUND HOUSE TAVERN, CLIFTON ROAD, BRIGHOUSE

A medium visited the family who lived at the Round House Tavern in 1996, when the licensee and his son saw a ghostly old man in the cellars. This is a listed building which was once used as a cell for prisoners kept in custody at a former police station in nearby Lawson Road.

Mr Barraclough said:

I got a very cold feeling down in the cellar and I saw this dark shadow-like figure. Then my nine-year-old son Nicky saw the same thing. While running up the stairs from the cellar he turned round and saw it again. He was absolutely petrified and was in tears for about half an hour afterwards. He was terrified.

When the medium Janet Bibby called to investigate, she sensed a heavy atmosphere on entering the cellar; she was able to describe the ghost as 'Walter', a little man with a gaunt face who never wanted to harm anyone.

Said Mrs Bibby:

I lit a candle, stood up a wooden cross, sat on a stool and prayed. As soon as he realised I would do him no harm he came to the front. I could see he was scared and worried, and needed to go into God's light. I asked God if he would take this man into his light and out of his misery.

The Blue Ball Inn, Soyland. The author's dad, Jack Owens, is pictured standing outside the inn, which is reputed to be haunted by a man with a black beard.

The room then lit up, and when I had finished praying, I knew everything was alright because there was a different atmosphere, and I got a different feeling. It was beautiful to know his soul had gone to rest.

BLUE BALL, SOYLAND

There has been a pub on this site since Roman times, since it was a convenient place for legions to rest on their long marches from Chester to York. Although the inn has its legends, the modern ghost story relates to the occasional sightings of a man in the bar area.

In 1991, a part-time barman, Phil Chappell, told how he was enjoying a quiet drink last thing at night with the licensee Rose Foster, after the last customers had left the building.

He said:

I was just sitting there talking and I saw this man standing by the bar and leaning against the wall. He was balding and had a black beard, wearing an open-necked shirt and a black jacket. He just looked straight at me and smiled.

As Mr Chappell looked on, the man just disappeared. The barman joked, 'I just thought he could have bought me a pint while he was here!'

nine

HAUNTED HALLS

SHIBDEN HALL

Shibden Hall is a grand old Hall overlooking a beautiful public park of the same name, and dates from 1420. It is a mystery as to what exactly stalks its ancient walls, though several members of staff have stated that there is definitely something there.

Tony Sharpe, an attendant at the Hall for twenty-six years, told the BBC website:

> You see things out of the corner of your eye. I've heard noises. You hear creaks and groans (I put them down to my knees now!), but it is a different atmosphere at night. It's completely different if you have to stay over. I once spent six nights here by myself and it was a different world, a different atmosphere altogether. Spooky stuff, but it's just something that people who work there have to get used to. I know that the former curator once said she had seen a cat walk through the wall of her office. Now she's a fully qualified vicar, so she wasn't making it up!
>
> I've never seen any figures, but I've heard voices and I've heard footsteps. We smell lavender and also fresh pipe tobacco as if someone's just lit up a pipe… at the cellar head and at the bottom of the tower as well. Then you go back and it's gone.
>
> The worst thing that happened to me was earlier this year (2007). I was opening the side gate and it was dark – about half-past-seven in the morning. I was suddenly aware of this big black shape above the left of my head. There was definitely something there. It was weird. It wasn't a bird or anything like that, it was just like a big black cloak. It was quite frightening.

Despite this unnerving episode, Tony Sharpe is sure there is nothing malevolent here, only something unexplained:

> I do feel there's something, but it's in the fabric of the building – the people who've lived here for 600 years or so. I think they've left something in the building itself. I'm not saying there are poltergeists or anything like that, but it's definitely an atmosphere. It's not a bad one, though. I think it was a happy house!

Shibden Hall, Halifax. The spectre of John Lister revels in breaking the anti-smoking laws: staff have smelt smoke from his pipe, plus the aroma of lavender. (Courtesy of Linda Hall)

East Riddlesden Hall, Keighley is a possible contender for the title of the most haunted house in West Yorkshire.

EAST RIDDLESDEN HALL, KEIGHLEY

There have been numerous press reports about Riddlesden, with headlines like 'Riddled with Ghosts', and many books on the subject have included whole chapters about this beautiful old Hall. Although it dates from the 1640s, and was built by James Murgatroyd, two Tudor houses originally stood on the site, and there is historic evidence of a Saxon settlement here. The estate is also mentioned in the Domesday Book.

One report featured the testimony of Ms Ana Chylak, who had worked as property manager at the Hall for six-and-a-half years. Although she recalled a number of anecdotes from colleagues and visitors, she remained largely sceptical of Riddlesden's traditional phantom – that of the Grey Lady. The story goes that the husband of the Grey Lady discovered her in bed with her lover and so locked her away to starve to death, and then walled up her lover in another part of the house. She is now apparently seen wandering the corridors looking for him. Although sceptical of the legend, Ms Chylak was more convinced about more modern-day happenings.

In the reception area, things have fallen off shelves and lights have switched themselves on; people have been tripped up in the shop and someone was pushed downstairs. In the Great Hall, a man had to leave when he was almost deafened by the sound of a wild party, which no one else could hear; in the Great Chamber, items put on the bed tend to fall off or break when left unattended; a little girl in a blue dress has also been seen crying nearby.

There is another old story of how a Scottish merchant was murdered at the Hall in 1790. The steward put him up for the night, and gave him food and drink, but killed him and stole his money. Although this tale is less well-known, it has been verified as it was recorded in contemporary newspapers, and it has links to the paranormal: a psychic had the sensation of being stabbed in the back when he visited the Bothy about three years ago, as if picking up on a psychic echo of the murder.

Ms Chylak also discussed the singing voices which have been reported in the tea room. She told the paper, 'Unseen children have been heard singing "Ring-a-Ring-a-Roses". The ladies who work there have heard it quite often. They heard it in December 2000.'

However, she has experienced something herself at the foot of the attic stairs, as she was closing curtains and locking up one night. She said:

Stupidly, I switched off all the electric lights before I went upstairs. I got to the bottom of the attic stairs, when suddenly there was an overpowering scent of Frankincense. I thought 'I don't like this', so I slammed the last door and went downstairs.

She put the experience out of her mind until last year when she was showing a group of teachers around the Hall, and one of them had the same experience. 'I like to have a rational explanation for things. Old houses creak and crack when they heat up and cool down, and I feel it is a friendly house.'

Some years ago, it was reported that two previously unknown ghosts had been sighted by a visitor to the Hall. Charles Fletcher, of Manchester, had been enjoying a wedding reception at the Hall. He popped outside just before midnight, and spotted two strange figures wearing long dark dresses hobbling along 20ft from him, and 'wondered what they were doing at such a late time.'

The women, around 5ft and 4ft 2inch tall, passed straight through a chain in front of the building and disappeared into the Hall through the thick stone wall. 'I was absolutely flabbergasted. I went forward to see if there was some opening but all I could see was the wall.'

He asked staff if they knew whom the figures were. At first they thought he had been seeing things after drinking, but, as Mr Fletcher pointed out, he had been drinking tonic water all night because he was driving.

House steward Michael Freeman was quoted as saying that, judging by where they disappeared, the two figures pre-date the Hall, as ghosts normally pass through old doorways, and none existed where the couple passed through.

He said:

It suggests the two figures are from an earlier period and are walking into a previous building or on what was open ground. With a thousand years of history on the site, there is bound to be something, and this must have been an echo of the past.

BOLLING HALL

Bolling Hall is apparently the oldest building in Bradford. It was mentioned in the Domesday Book, written after the Norman invasion of 1066, and since then has had a multitude of owners. It had previously belonged to a Saxon, but was given to a Norman knight named Ilbert De Laci, as a reward for his services to the King – William the Conqueror.

Bolling boasts one of the most widely known ghost stories in Yorkshire. While planning the siege of Bradford during the English Civil War, the Earl of Newcastle, a commander of the Royalist forces, is said to have ordered his men to kill all the townspeople. However, that night he was awakened by the spirit of a girl pleading him to 'Pity poor Bradford'. Chilled to the bone, and afraid of disobeying, he changed his orders in the morning and only ten armed men in Bradford were killed in the fighting.

However, I learned that there were many different experiences of a wide variety of alleged ghosts reported by successive owners of the Hall, right up to the present day, so I decided to find out more.

Liz McIvor, the curator of the museum in August 2005, said that she and other curators had kept records of scores of sightings of ghosts. However, letters and correspondents from those who have stayed at the house show that ghosts have been sighted throughout its history.

In the late 1800s, a servant was preparing to meet her paramour in the gardens when she spotted a large gathering of silent cavalier soldiers riding across the grass.

Miss McIvor said:

> We've had visions of everything from medieval ghosts up to a woman dressed in 1960s clothing. Strange things do happen and for there to have been so many people reporting seeing things throughout hundreds of years here it makes me think there is something in it.

In the past, the events have proved too much for some staff. The museum had five nightwatchmen in just three years.

The most common ghost is that of Caroline Wood. Mrs Wood, as she is known to staff, lived in the Hall during the late-eighteenth and early nineteenth centuries, and is sighted throughout the house and in particular in the room where her portrait hangs.

One of those to see her is Paul Hodgson, who said:

> We had just closed up and I was doing some vacuuming. For some reason I stopped for a moment and looked across the hall where I saw a lady standing there looking towards me. She was only there for about three seconds before she disappeared into the stairs but it came as quite a shock.

Paul has his own theory about the ghosts. 'I think they are watching over us to make sure the house is looked after.'

BAILDON HALL

Baildon Hall is a fifteenth-century manor house, though part of it dates back as far as 1300, and it belonged to the Baildon family from 1408. Today it's a social club owned by Baildon Hall Co. Ltd.

Bolling Hall, Bradford; more than just an old legend haunts here. (Courtesy of Linda Hall)

Margaret Ludkin catches an 'orb' at Bolling Hall. (Courtesy of Margaret Ludkin)

It stands on Hallfield Drive in Baildon, just past the turn-off to Station Road. Once a grand manor house, Baildon Hall used to look out over fields, and the owners also owned Baildon cottages. However, these have long since been demolished, to be replaced with modern residences.

President of the club Barbara Boyes is also the Hall's historian, and she kindly invited me for a visit and a chat about the Hall's spectral history. She told me that ghostly sights and sounds are commonplace, and until recently no one had dared to spend a night at the Hall.

She says, 'doors open and close, balls roll across the snooker table upstairs when there's nobody there, lightbulbs fall out of their sockets and beer glasses fly off shelves.'

Barbara has been a member of the club for around twenty years. She has been president for the last four, and her husband Keith has been the club's treasurer for the last twelve. He often works alone in the Hall at night. He told journalist Emma Claydon of the newspaper *Telegraph & Argus*, 'I've seen a man sitting in a chair, then suddenly he's gone. I've tripped on the stairs and felt something touch my neck. I've heard footsteps. You get used to it.'

When I visited, Barbara and Keith had just completed the refurbishment of the room above the main lounge, where the band hold rehearsals, after the room had lain in rubble and dormant for sixty years. They had gained a grant to help with the expense, but club members had raised the rest of the funding themselves.

Barbara researched the Hall's history and says that the most popular theory about the ghost's identity is Francis Baildon, who died there in 1669. She says:

> He had gambling debts and was on the point of losing his home. He became mysteriously ill, and his wife, Jane Hawksworth of Hawksworth Hall, along with their daughter and her husband, sold his cattle at markets then removed his belongings. Francis may have been poisoned by his family and abandoned on his deathbed.

The ghost or ghosts may have been around for centuries, but there are no records relating early experiences; all of the recorded happenings date from relatively recent times.

There used to be a snooker table in the bar. One customer was playing alone and put his empty pint glass on the side of the table. Looking away for a moment, he was astonished to turn back and find the glass had turned itself upside down!

Baildon Hall, near Bradford, where the ghosts of a man in a chair and a monk by the fireplace have been spotted.

Barbara showed me a tiny back room, which is used as an office, where Keith saw a man sitting in a chair. He vanished immediately, but the same thing happened again a fortnight later. Barbara describes her husband as a down-to-earth and matter-of-fact sort of man, and that if he says something happened, then it happened.

One evening, while in the building alone, Keith was upstairs in the current snooker room. He found a cue which a player had left leaning against the wall and he replaced it in the cue rack. As he did so, Keith got a distinctly odd feeling that there was someone else in the room – when he knew there wasn't. He turned to see a monk standing in the corner next to an old fireplace. In an instant, he had gone, but the apparition was accompanied by the sound of very loud organ music, which gradually faded away. 'He got home pretty quick that evening!' joked Barbara.

On my visit to the Hall, one of the cleaners related to me how she thought she saw someone walk through the back door and along the length of the wall in the lounge and bar area, and assumed it was the steward – until the steward appeared at her side from the other direction. 'How did you get back round here so quickly?' she asked. He didn't understand what she was talking about, as he had only just entered the building. The cleaner also saw a monk standing just behind the bar, who was gone a few seconds later.

Barbara agrees that these phenomena tend to happen to people who are not looking for them. Most witnesses are people just going about their day-to-day duties.

Barbara was sitting alone in the bar one day, while Keith was upstairs, when the CD player behind the bar switched itself on and started playing very loud music. Barbara recalled:

> We never used the player when we were alone in the building, so it made me jump even more. I ran upstairs to my husband and told him what had happened.
>
> In the Oak Room there was an old chest, on which stood a vase of daffodils. I went to get some more, and when I returned, the vase had gone. I searched high and low for them and eventually found them over the other side of the room. No one else had been in that room during the time I had been away, and I thought, 'Am I seeing things? Had I moved them, then forgotten about it?' But I knew I hadn't.

In March 2006, an investigation was staged at the Hall in the presence of a television company who were hoping to sell the programme on the internet. If it was ever shown, the owners of the Hall never got to hear about it. Around thirty people took part in the investigation including three mediums, one of whom picked up on an apparent ghost, previously not known, which led to another intriguing discovery about the Hall's history.

The aptly named medium Mark Waldspirit picked up on a woman's presence. He said, 'She was tumbling downstairs. She looked like a maid. I know nothing about this place. I always start with a clean slate. All I know is that there are many centuries of history here – and buildings absorb emotions.' Barbara told me that this revelation was very, very strange.

> When I was researching the book, I read that one of the lords of the manor had been hanged at York for murdering a sheriff's officer. However, I was reading a book by Dr John Simpson, written in around 1800, which quoted someone who said he had been up to Baildon to discuss the lord of the manor – who had been hanged at York for murdering a maidservant here.

Barbara had a visit from an architect, who was also psychic. He sensed it was a friendly place with nothing frightening or evil about it.

Val, one of the cleaners, told me:

> I was cleaning the room where the band practice, next to the snooker room, and I left the thru-door open as I worked. All of a sudden the door banged shut and I'm sure I heard the sound of somebody giggling. The door banged shut for no reason at all, and there was nobody else there.

Barbara recounted other happenings to me, including the shattering of silver plates which were hurled right across to the other side of the kitchen, landing in the sink. Doors open and shut of their own accord.

Says Barbara:

> We were sitting in the lounge having a coffee when the door from the kitchen opened very slowly, stayed open, then closed again very slowly, just as if someone had walked in!
>
> Similarly, on another occasion, Keith and three friends were sitting at a table near the side door – which is very heavy and does not blow open in the wind – when it opened and closed. They all peered round the corner expecting to see someone – and, again, there was no one there.

So what does Barbara think ghosts are? Some unknown branch of science, or life after death, or another explanation?

> I don't know, I've not experienced anything myself. Well, apart from the doors opening and shutting, that sort of thing. But I've not seen anything. But there's something here. There's no doubt about that. It's something unexplainable.

ten

A GAGGLE OF GHOSTS

HEATH FARM, WAKEFIELD

Jackie and Graham Johnson moved into Heath Farm in 1991 and were interviewed in the mystery magazine *Fortean Times* about the multitude of phenomena which they have experienced here.

The property sits on the Dewsbury to Wakefield Road in the picturesque village of Heath which, as the name suggests, possesses a large heath, together with a village pub and lovely houses. The farm itself dates from the seventeenth century and was built on a network of mining tunnels.

The couple have seen various apparitions on the property, including an elderly woman, dressed in an apron, apparently feeding the chickens! A corner of the farm's workshop is the spot where the ghost of an old man has been seen: he has been blamed for switching off the lights and the machinery at exactly 3.30 p.m. every day. Workers from a double-glazing company were spooked by the old man, who appeared from nowhere and sat watching them at work, before suddenly vanishing when he was approached by one of the men.

Other hauntings and happenings include the ghost of a man with a shotgun who stalks the perimeter of the property; a group of children, thought to be plague victims; and a woman who cries for her child in the kitchen.

Poltergeist-type phenomena has been reported with objects such as money, keys and pens appearing and disappearing. A ghostly voice which calls people's names for no apparent reason has been heard, and phrases such as 'call the dog' or 'call the horse' have been heard echoing across the farmyard, when there is no one there to account for them.

PHANTOM RIDER

Rodney G. Hallam has always been a keen walker and on this particular day, around 1990-1992, he was climbing Beckfoot Lane, near Bingley. He said:

Heath Farm, the haunt of at least three ghosts.

Beckfoot Lane, Bingley, home to a phantom horseman.

I walked up the lane towards the stream where the road narrows, just before the old bridge, when I saw a man on horseback on the side of the road. He was about 10-15ft away from me, and dressed in what I would describe as a Tudor costume from the period of Elizabeth I.

As I stared at him, I thought I had arrived on the set of some film or television programme, and I looked around for the television crew and cameras, but there was no one else there. I did not talk to the man or wave to him, and he totally ignored me, looking straight ahead. I was somewhat embarrassed as I did not want to spoil what I took to be part of the production's shooting. I continued up the hill, searching in vain for a film unit, but there was no sign of anyone else.

If I had thought for a moment that he was an apparition I would certainly have spoken to him. However, I didn't know this, and as I walked past him, I did not turn to look at him again, as I was intent on continuing to walk up the lane to see if there were any more 'actors' or television/film crew. I was somewhat disappointed when I saw no one else on my walk up the lane to St Ives.

It suddenly began to dawn on me that I had seen a ghost. Years later, I shared this experience with a friend who lived in the Shipley area, who said to me: 'Oh, have you seen him too?'

I would be pleased to learn more of this apparition if anyone can help.

The old cemetery, Shipley – beware the phantom Medallion Man!

Shipley Glen. (Courtesy of Mike Hall)

MEDALLION MAN

There is an old cemetery in Shipley, just outside Bradford, no longer in use, says Mrs Kathleen Cliff. It is completely hidden from view behind a bank of trees on Briggate, near the railway.

In June or July 2002, Mrs Cliff's thirteen-year-old daughter took a friend to the cemetery who wanted to look around it, but when her daughter returned she was white-faced and frightened. She told her mother how a man had appeared in front of her wearing strange clothes and a medallion-type chain around his neck. Then he vanished.

Mrs Cliff wonders if this may have been the ghost of a former Lord Mayor of Bradford, and added that it would be interesting to look up old records to see if such a person had been buried in the cemetery. Needless to say, her daughter has not revisited the cemetery since that day.

Clay House, West Vale, where Jayne Hewitt saw a man hanging from a tree on the driveway.

CLAY HOUSE, WEST VALE

Many years ago, I received a letter from a Ms Jayne Hewitt, of Huddersfield, who used to live at West Vale, near Greetland in Halifax.

She was in the habit of walking her dog after work, but this evening she was home a little later. It was winter and a very dark evening when she turned the corner on the main road and walked up the driveway to Clay House.

As she neared the old house, she got a strange sensation – a feeling that something wasn't quite right – and looked to her left (where there are several trees which skirt the narrow driveway) to see the image of a man hanging from a branch on one of the trees.

'It was only for a split-second and then it was gone, but I was absolutely certain of what I saw.' Unsurprisingly, she turned and ran back home and never ventured up the driveway after dark again!

BBC RADIO LEEDS

Studio 2 at Broadcasting House, on Woodhouse Lane, is notorious as the spot where the Grey Lady has been, and, in earlier years, a monk-like figure, and there have been many eyewitnesses.

In the 1930s, when the BBC took over the building, members of staff were constantly reporting the form of a hooded figure, like a monk, gliding across the gallery into Studio 2 – passing straight through the wall!

Former employee Albert Aldred worked there during the Second World War, and he told of how he would often hear the sound of footsteps late at night when there was no one else in the building, pacing the gallery which leads to the newsroom near Studio 2. He told the author and psychical researcher Terence Whitaker that many employees did not like working there alone at night as a result and some even resigned from their jobs through fear.

BBC Radio Leeds. A ghostly figure is said to haunt the gallery near Studio 2.

Poltergeist activity has also been reported in the building. One Sunday evening in December 1978, receptionist Sharon Carter was sitting in the restroom on the first floor chatting to a friend on the telephone when she felt the temperature suddenly drop; she carried the telephone across the room where it seemed warmer and continued with the conversation. Suddenly, there was a resounding crash, and as she turned, Sharon saw that a kettle, which had been on the floor, had floated through the air and smashed into the sink. She fled from the room and refused to return.

Although the ghost of Studio 2 has not actually been seen in recent years, the sensation of being watched by an unseen presence is a very real phenomenon, experienced by many people up to the present day.

One employee used to play the piano in Studio 2, and would often hear a strange sound, as if someone was humming and whistling along in musical accompaniment. Whenever she stopped playing, the sound would continue for a short while and then stop. It then began again when she continued. Another employee recalled how he always took the long way round when he was the first to arrive in the morning, consciously steering clear of Studio 2.

No one seems to know the reason behind the supposed haunting, but many people know it is not just part of the imagination. There really is something that stalks Studio 2, both day and night.

GREENFIELD LODGE, BARKISLAND

Greenfield Lodge is a large Georgian building in the remote village of Barkisland in Calderdale, which has fifteen bedrooms, with a courtyard plus a barn and stables.

A range of unusual auditory phenomena have been reported by previous owners – the sound of a woman's muffled voice, a car pulling up outside when there are no vehicles in the vicinity, plus loud bumps and crashes coming from empty rooms.

When any changes to the structure of the building have been carried out, a woman in a high-necked blouse and a long grey skirt, thought to be a previous owner, Elizabeth Emmett,

Greenfield Lodge, Barkisland.

The Brontë parsonage, Haworth. Do the spectres of the Brontës' haunt here and the nearby moors?

The sign at the Brontë parsonage.

Haworth Church, opposite the parsonage.

appears in the Lodge and is always weeping – apparently not a fan of DIY! However, the most intriguing ghostly encounters have occurred on the outside of the building.

One woman, who used to deliver milk to the Lodge, recalled how she felt that someone was sitting in the passenger seat of her car as she pulled up outside the Lodge, and was gobsmacked as the invisible occupant opened the door to climb out and shut it again!

The other 'open air' spooks have woken up successive owners in the middle of the night. One owner was awoken by the sound of children playing on the road outside in the middle of the night, and peered out to see a group of boys running around the forecourt. They ran off towards a nearby pub, then returned and gradually faded away!

A particularly intriguing experience happened to the previous owners one night. They were awoken by the screech of brakes outside and as they peered through the curtains, they saw a woman sitting in a car and a man checking the fastenings on the gate of the Lodge. The owners heard the woman shriek to the man, 'Come on, let's get out of here!' Then she pointed to the Lodge and said, 'It came from in there!' The man rejoined her in the car, and they drove off quickly. The owners had often wondered exactly what 'it' was, and what had scared the couple so much.

HAUNTED HAWORTH

Much has been written about the Brontës, for they have made the little town of Haworth the tourist success it is today. The preserved cobbled main street, standing defiantly in a sea of modern semi-detached and terraces, and perched on the edge of the moors leading to Top Withens and the village of Stanbury, are part and parcel of the history that the Brontë legacy has left us.

Haworth also has its fair share of ghost and hauntings, most of them centred around the main street, the moors, the village church and the parsonage. Those who possess that strange 'second sight', sensitive to moods and atmospheres, have also recounted how they have picked up on the otherworldly vibrations that have somehow been embedded into the fabric of the buildings and grounds of the village. In his fascinating book *Hauntings in Yorkshire*, Steven Wade recounts the various reports of hauntings in the area including the solitary ghost who walks between the parsonage and Top Withens, where Emily used to walk, deep in thought, as she planned her various writings. Other haunted locations include the parsonage and churchyard, together with the Toby Jug restaurant, whose owner has contacted local papers to tell them of Emily's various ghostly appearances in the building. Steve Wade himself recounts how he saw a black dog – not the fearsome, Baskerville-type black hound Guytrash, which is woven into Yorkshire folklore, but an ordinary-looking dog which '…slinked across the road by the Black Bull in front of me as I returned from (my) walk from Stanbury. It dissolved into a wall.' This is one of the several episodes which Steve has experienced during his researches, many of which he recounts in his intriguing volume.

SOUTHOWRAM WESLEYAN METHODIST CHURCH

I came across a news cutting from the *Evening Courier*, in Halifax, dating from 1973, which reported how a Mr Derek Rhodes had filmed his niece's wedding at the Wesleyan Methodist church in Southowram, near the town. He stood on the balcony in the gallery pointing his viewfinder at the proceedings below and could see nothing amiss. However, on viewing the tape he saw a woman dressed in black, with a veil over her face, mingling amongst the guests.

He made enquiries to the church steward and asked all the guests at the wedding and no one could recall seeing her, which is strange as the church is quite small and the woman would have stood out amongst the well-wishers, as her attire seemed more in tune with a funeral than a wedding.

However, according to Mr Rhodes, the figure appears to be speaking and then simply fades away on video! This sounds too good to be true and, although I made enquiries when I came across the cutting, I could not locate Mr Rhodes nor his niece and family so, unfortunately, I cannot vouch for the story. If any readers think they can help please get in touch with me, c/o my publishers.

LONG CAN, OVENDEN WOOD, HALIFAX

This former visitors' centre for Webster's Brewery was built in 1637 as a row of terraced houses by the noted architect James Murgatroyd. In many reported cases of hauntings, building work seems to be the cause of phenomena, which only occurs after structural work is carried out such as removing walls, replacing staircases, etc. And while there are no early records indicating if the ghostly happenings occurred here in earlier centuries, staff at Long Can only began to experience them only after the renovation work had begun.

Ms Sarah Thornton worked as catering manageress from 1987, and her duties included preparing buffet lunches for the visitors. On several occasions, she heard doors open followed by the sound of footsteps, when she was alone in the building. On one occasion, she felt so unnerved by it that she asked a security guard to accompany her until the guests arrived. She felt a little foolish mentioning it to the kitchen staff but many of them had also experienced it too.

One waitress told Ms Thornton how she had been browsing the museum part of the building, in which there are display cabinets containing various objects such as old boots and clothes, discovered by workmen during their renovation work, when she got the sensation that there was someone standing behind her. The waitress spun round and was just in time to catch the image of an elderly woman in a long grey dress falling downwards as if through the floorboards. The waitress recalled how she was shivering when she left the museum.

I have also met Howard Maude, the former host of Long Can, who was also in charge of the bar and the cellar, who had his own odd experiences there. The thing that he most often noticed was the curious aroma of eggs and bacon which wafted through the bar and cellar even when the kitchen was not in use. He later discovered that the cellar used to be the kitchen in the middle cottage before the conversion.

When Long Can reopened following a bank holiday, Howard was amazed to find that the objects in the display case in the museum had been neatly relocated from the top shelf to the bottom shelf of the cabinet, although there was no physical way this could have been achieved without unlocking the cabinet. Only the security department had the keys, and they had not been anywhere near it.

Southowram Church, where a lady in black was apparently caught on video.

Long Can, where phantom footsteps have been heard and where the Grey Lady is said to roam.

Cleaners at Long Can have told of being tapped on the shoulder in the toilets, then turning round to find no one there, and also glimpsing a white figure out of the corner of the eye, as if someone has rushed past quickly, when there is a no one else in the vicinity.

CITY VARIETIES THEATRE, LEEDS

Several ghosts haunt the City Varieties Theatre in Leeds. The author Terence Whitaker interviewed television producer Len Marten who went to see a revue performed at the theatre many years ago and found himself accidentally locked in by the staff. Not knowing what to do, he sat on a seat in the bar area by a log fire and fell asleep. He awoke sometime later to find that the room had become extremely chilly. Looking up, he saw a lady in a crinoline dress sitting by the fireplace and looking directly at him. As he cried out in shock, the woman turned to the fireplace and disappeared through it, as did the chilly atmosphere, and the room warmed up again. He testified that she seemed real and solid, which added to his shock when she walked straight through the fireplace! To make matters worse, he had to sit in the darkness and wait for the nightwatchman to make his rounds before he could get out of the building.

When Jim McNish visited the theatre in June 1983 as part of a course in stage design, he and several other students were given a tour of the theatre. The theatre employee who showed

City Varieties Theatre, Leeds. A room is kept locked from visitors…

them around recounted details of the various hauntings associated with the theatre, including the 'evil' atmosphere which pervaded a room at the back of the auditorium, between the lighting operator's booth and the entrance to the bar. The door had a heavy padlock on it, and they were told that none of the employee's would enter there, because of the unnerving sensation.

Mr McNish asked for the keys and entered the room. It was completely empty with gaping holes in the rotting floorboards. Although there was no lightswitch, there were many slates missing from the roof and the bright summer's day beamed in providing enough light for him to see where he was going. There was a ladder propped up against the rafters and the man climbed the first two rungs. He said:

> As I looked into the rafters, I suddenly felt incredibly cold. My guts flip-flopped like I was on a roller-coaster, all my hair stood on end and my heart started pumping at 200 beats-per-minute. I could not get out of that room quick enough!

Once outside, he expected his waiting friends to laugh at him and his reaction, but they had also sensed the atmosphere.

He never returned to the theatre but, many years later, he still wondered if it was a real ghostly presence or simply a psychological reaction to being told about the atmosphere. Whatever the truth, the sensation at the time seemed very real and abnormal to him.

LEEDS COMBINED COURTS

The site which currently houses Leeds Combined Courts in the city centre has also previously been a fire station, a police station and a row of terraced houses, originally constructed in 1815.

Sightings persist of an elderly, balding man in a grey suit, who is seen crouching in the corner of one of the courtrooms, bending over in the car park and walking down corridors,

Leeds Combined
Courts, the haunt
of an elderly man
in a grey suit.

particularly first thing in the morning and last thing at night. It is hardly surprising, therefore, that most of the eyewitnesses are security guards. The man was seen one morning as a guard was unlocking the main entrance, though an immediate search failed to reveal any sign of him. The guard was so spooked by the incident that he will no longer approach that area. A female security guard, however, was intrigued to see the man walking hurriedly down a corridor and watched him turn a corner which led into a courtroom. However, when the guard entered the room there was no sign of the man, and all the other entrances and exits to the courtroom were securely locked.

THE WATCHER IN THE NIGHT

I have heard accounts of people witnessing a variety of phenomena in the house they lived in, but one source, who I shall call Lindsay, recounts how she experienced identical phenomena in three *different* homes. It seemed to follow her wherever she moved!

Says Lindsay:

Having got married in the summer of 1982, my husband and myself moved into rented accommodation, as we hadn't got enough money saved for a deposit on a house. The house, situated on May Street, at Crosland Moor, Huddersfield, was a normal terraced house, nothing special, basic but clean. It had a cellar, a living room with kitchenette, bathroom, one bedroom and a large attic. I never had any 'strange' feelings about the house and nor did my husband ever mention that he had.

We had been living there for about six months, when, one night, my husband went to the local pub with his brother and I had decided to have an early night which, for me, was around 10.30 p.m.

I'm not sure how long I had been asleep, but was woken by what I thought was my husband moving in the corner of the bedroom. I just thought the person I saw was him getting undressed in the dark, and I then went back to sleep. Some time later, I was awoken by the bedroom door opening and a figure coming in. I recall yelling something like, 'Who is it?' It turned out to be my husband, who said, 'It's only me.'

I told him I had already seen him earlier in the bedroom, but we both put it down to me having a dream. Some weeks later, a similar thing happened, but the figure was standing near the bedroom door and it soon vanished. I saw the man maybe two or three more times whilst we lived at that property. He was always standing by the bedroom door looking towards the bed, and always faded within a few seconds of me waking.

Within about a year we'd moved into a nice little house which we had bought. Again, nothing special: a two-bedroom terrace on Lightcliffe Road, at Crosland Moor, Huddersfield, but it was ours.

I remember the first time I saw the man again. I awoke in the middle of the night. I don't know what woke me, but there he was, this time at my side of the bed, near the bottom. Forgetting about the other house, I panicked, thinking there was an intruder. I shouted this to my husband. I was the first to get out of bed, and watched the figure leave by the bedroom door, which was always wide open. We ran to the landing and put on the lights, but no one was there. We searched the house, checking all the doors and windows (which were locked), but no one was there.

Over the months, this happened again and again, probably a couple of times a month. My husband never saw the figure and came to the conclusion that I was losing my marbles!

As the months became years, I'd got used to this figure coming to see me and realised if I didn't panic, and just lay there quietly, I could watch him watching me. It was as if he would go away if he knew I was awake, but if he thought I was asleep, he would stay.

In 1992, I got divorced and moved into a flat until the house was sold and I could find one of my own to buy, this time situated on Ruth Street, at Newsome, Huddersfield. I was there for about sixteen months and in that time saw the figure, always standing at the bottom of my bed, on several occasions. However, on one occasion I got up to go to the bathroom, then went to the kitchen for a drink. I didn't put any lights on, but there he was in the living room. From where he was standing, you could see into the bedroom where I was sleeping. He turned and disappeared.

In 1993, I bought my own little house, which I was very proud of. Over the weeks when I was settling in, I wondered if I would see the figure who had been watching over me for the last ten years, but he never appeared to me again.

The figure was male, dressed in dark trousers and top. Slim physique. Although I never saw his face, my impression was he was aged between twenty-five and forty. He never spoke. I never heard spooky noises. If you can imagine someone standing in a dark room, with the only light coming through the closed curtains, at night-time – that's the only way I can describe it.

About six months after I moved into my house, I was listening to a radio programme and people were calling in to discuss their ghostly experiences. This young woman called in and began describing the exact same experience as I had – but the irony is, she said this visitor began visiting her about six months ago, around the time I had moved. She described this man exactly and how he stood in her bedroom.

In the years since, I've often thought about this man: what did he want and why me? It became a comfort to me at night-time to know he was there. I am a level-headed and open-minded person, but I have often wondered if he was a guardian angel.

FLOCKTON, NEAR WAKEFIELD

A local policeman, who prefers to remain anonymous, has told of seeing strangers walk past him at the dead of night. Wondering if they are would-be burglars seeking a prospective house to break into, he has turned back to keep a close watch on them, to find they have disappeared! It would be interesting to know if anyone else in that area has witnessed the same phenomenon.

THE PRIESTLEY CENTRE FOR THE ARTS, BRADFORD

They say that every good theatre has a ghost, and The Priestley is no exception. Irene Lofthouse, funding co-ordinator, kindly invited me along for a tour of this lovely old building and also filled me in on the ghostly goings-on regularly experienced here:

> A woman in seat H18 appears when the dress circle is empty. We still sell tickets for that seat and nobody sitting there has said they felt a presence, but the woman has certainly been seen by several people from the stage.
>
> Then there's the man in the top hat and cloak who's been spotted several times making his way across the foyer. Several people have heard giggling – when the theatre is empty – and in the bar there are often cases of people seeing something out the corner of their eye, then when they look again, there's nobody there.

Irene has felt a presence in the wardrobe department, a series of rooms that are home to hundreds of old costumes, some of them dating back more than a century. 'I've felt a cold spot appear then quickly disappear. Several people have felt that in wardrobe. It's not a threatening feeling; you just get a chill down the spine.'

After our chat, Irene led me on a ghost tour of The Priestley, recounting the multitude of phenomena which have been experienced here. In a corner of the bar, several members of the theatre regularly see things moving around such as vague shapes, odd lights and brief shadows as if someone has just walked past.

Flockton, near Wakefield. Do ghostly pedestrians wander the main street at night?

The Priestly Centre for the Arts, where a shadowy figure has been seen sitting in seat H18.

Irene continues:

In the other corner of the bar, one man in particular has been pushed in the back on several occasions, while he has been sitting with others round a table discussing business matters with the Board. Strangely, he is the only person to have experienced this. And we don't know why!

The foyer is the scene of the most regularly sighted ghost: a tall man in a top hat and dark coat who climbs the staircase, turning left to the foyer, walking past the reception desk and straight through the closed door opposite! However, witnesses can only clearly see the top half of the man. His legs are partly missing – and the theory to account for this is that the current floor level has been raised higher than it was when this man was still alive.

As the tour drew to close, Irene told me:

There are no unpleasant happenings here. All the presences are fairly benign, but it can be frustrating and baffling nonetheless, particularly last thing at night when you go round checking that all the lights in the building are switched off. You're the last one in the building and you leave – only to find that one of the lights is still on! And you think, 'How can that light still be on?' You know full well that you switched them all off. The basement lights, particularly, tend to switch themselves on even when no one has been down there for a week!

eleven

A DOLL'S HOUSE

A lady who prefers to remain anonymous, and whom I shall call 'Joan', wrote to me after reading my previous book *Haunted Bradford*. What really intrigued Joan about the book was a reference I had made to a private house on the Pollard Park estate, in Bradford, which was reported to have been haunted. I didn't know exactly which building it was, and Joan made enquiries, but could not find the exact flat. However, she believed the Pollard Park ghost to be her late husband's Aunt Frances, who used to live there, and who, according to Joan, was a rather formidable woman. Joan has also experienced some ghostly activity which she believes could be Aunt Frances. I will let Joan tell her story in her own words:

After I retired from work, I decided to take up woodwork. I went to classes twice a week in Shipley. As I liked doll's houses, I decided to make a model of Arkwright's shop from the programme *Open All Hours*. I made the basic model at Shipley, then brought the unfinished shop home to work on the interior. I have a workbench in the basement of my home, which is my workshop.

I was able to copy the shop interior from watching the television series, but was stuck when it came to decorating the bedroom above the shop. I needed some old, faded and authentic-looking wallpaper. I looked at papers in DIY stores, but all had a modern 'finish' to them. One day, while up in the attic, I glanced at Aunt Frances' box. [Frances had first made this box to keep her 'bottom drawer' items, such as household items and reams of crocheting. Frances always prided herself on her crocheting prowess. The box was a huge affair – almost the size of a tea-chest. It had a hinged lid, stood on casters and was lined, both inside and out, with old wallpaper. She was always very proud of this box and its contents.] There, decorating the box, was the perfect paper! I tried to loosen a bit but it was well and truly stuck so I brought up the wallpaper steamer stripper and it worked a treat. I carefully peeled back the wet pieces and I had enough to paper my model room. I also removed some of the old silver and white ceiling paper, until I had enough paper for Arkwright's ceiling. I took the pieces down into the basement to dry out for re-use. I returned upstairs and turned on the television. My husband was a shiftworker then and was at the late shift from 2 p.m.'til 9.30 p.m. It was getting late in the year and the nights were drawing in. It was dusk at the time, but not worth putting the lights on.

I can remember quite clearly the programme I was watching on television. It was a documentary about the building of skyscrapers in America. The television was situated in the right-hand fireside

Aunt Frances.

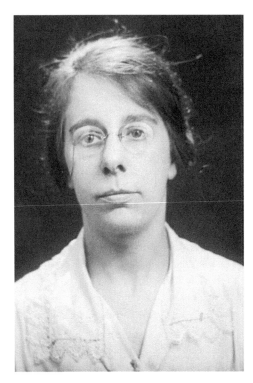

Aunt Frances.

The model of Arkwright's bedroom.

recess and Aunt Frances's aspidistra was in a pot on a low coffee table in the recess to the left. My programme had just reached the most interesting part… [when] my attention was suddenly diverted to the aspidistra in the corner, which started to shake of its own accord, which made all its leaves rustle! I could see it and I could hear it. It was exactly the same effect as if there was an earthquake just starting, as I had often seen on the films. This phenomena only lasted two or three seconds, but I definitely heard and saw what I did and had definitely not dropped off and dreamt it, as my husband always believed, and it was not a reflection from the television, because I both heard and saw it.

I knew I had seen something supernatural and was absolutely terrified and was riveted in my chair and could not move. It was as if, as some people describe, I was being held down in the chair. I am sure that it was not a heavy weight pinning me down (as some people say in the case of hauntings) – it was sheer terror which made me unable to move. The television was still switched on but I could not take my eyes off the plant. I dared not, I was waiting for it to happen again. The room started to get darker and darker and I wanted to get up and put the lights on, but I simply could not move. I'm not sure what I thought would happen to me if I did move, but I couldn't. Eventually, I made a dash for it. Jumped out of the chair, put the lights on and ran into the kitchen where I felt somehow safer. I could not bring myself to return to the living room. I went to the cupboard and got out the whisky bottle and poured myself a whisky then went to the telephone in the hall, sat at the foot of the staircase and rang my friend and neighbour just across the road. I told her what had happened and she actually did believe me – though I don't think I would have believed her in the same circumstances! But it was comforting just to be able to talk to someone.

I waited until nearly 9.30 p.m., then put on my coat and went to meet my husband from work, as I did not wish to be in the house alone. I told my husband of my experience but he never believed me and got quite angry every time I persisted. He said it was perfectly obvious that I had dozed off just when the programme mentioned earthquakes and had experienced a little momentary dream. I know this is not so. At this time, I made no connection between my experience and Aunt Frances.

On another occasion, I was alone in the basement working on my *Open All Hours'* shop and applying the paper in Arkwrights' bedroom, and my face was almost in the doll's house, when suddenly I heard a funny noise coming from the model. It was a sighing sort of noise, like the laboured deep breaths of someone in pain. I dropped whatever I was doing and shot up the cellar stairs. Later, I disbelieved myself, telling myself that what happened had been impossible. I did not tell my husband about that experience, as I knew he would not believe me as before.

It was not very long until I experienced another 'happening' – the most terrifying. I had a huge strong cardboard box in the basement with loads of other junk, and this was my scrapbox where I threw all the bits and pieces of wood in case they may come in handy for something, and it was almost full. It was the afternoon, my husband was at work and once again I was working on my model shop. Suddenly, everything in the cellar started to rattle; just a small rattle at first as if something had fallen over, but then it was as if everything started to join in! All the wood in the scrapbox started rattling, and all the tools everywhere were rattling and, most frightening of all, I could hear noises as if rubble and bits of masonry were falling between the cavity walls. This lasted longer than the aspidistra episode – about ten-fifteen seconds in all. I just sat on my chair (an old garden chair which I kept in the cellar), rigid and terrified. Eventually, after what seemed like hours, everything subsided and returned to normal – everything, that is, except me. Once my legs worked again, I did not know which way to run. Should I go to my right and up the cellar stairs, or grab the key from the shelf, unlock the cellar door and dash into the back garden? Eventually, I decided to make a bolt for the back garden, as I was afraid I might meet something on the cellar steps on my way up. I felt much better once I was outside, went out of the back gate and came back in the house via the front door which was, fortunately, unlocked.

Since then, I have had no more experiences with my project but I am convinced it was Aunt Frances haunting me for 'violating' her box. If anyone had told me that there had been an earthquake on these occasions, then that would have explained everything, but of course there was no earthquake reported – only inside my house.

I often think I must be one of the few people with a haunted doll's house!

BIBLIOGRAPHY

Bardens, Dennis, *Ghosts and Hauntings* (Senate/Random House, 1987)

Ellis, Chris and Owens, Andy, *Haunted Dorset* (SB Publicaions, 2004)

Heymer, John E., *The Entrancing Flame: The Facts of Spontaneous Human Combustion* (Little, Brown & Co., 1996)

Mackenzie, Andrew, *Hauntings and Apparitions* (William Heinemann, 1982)

Owens, Andy, *Haunted Bradford* (Tempus Publishing, 2007)

Owens, Andy, *Haunted Places of Yorkshire* (Countryside Books, 2005)

Owens, Andy, *Yorkshire Stories of the Supernatural* (Countryside Books, 1999)

Randles, Jenny, *The Pennine UFO Mystery* (Granada, 1983)

Randles, Jenny and Hough, Peter, *Spontaneous Human Combustion* (Robert Hale Ltd, 2007)

Spencer, John and Anne, *The Encyclopaedia of Ghosts and Spirits* (Headline, 1992)

Spencer, John and Anne, *The Encyclopaedia of Ghosts and Spirits: Volume Two* (Headline, 2001)

Wade, Stephen, *Hauntings in Yorkshire* (Halsgrove, 2008)

Whitaker, Terence W, *Northcountry Ghosts and Legends* (Grafton Books, 1988)

Wilson, Colin, *Poltergeist! A Study in Destructive Haunting* (New English Library, 1982)

Other titles published by The History Press

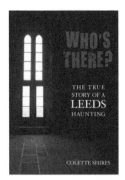

Who's There? The True Story of a Leeds Haunting
COLETTE SHIRES

When the Slater family heard what sounded like a baby crying in their new house, they had no idea that it was the beginning of a terrifying haunting that would last for more than thirty years, and follow them across the city. This is their story.

978 07524 4808 4

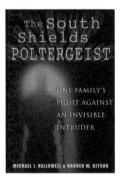

The South Shields Poltergeist: One Family's Fight Against An Invisible Intruder
MICHAEL J. HALLOWELL AND DARREN W. RITSON

Here is a chilling diary of an ongoing poltergeist case which rivals any previously documented. In December 2005, a family began to experience typical but low-level poltergeist-like phenomena in their home. Slowly but steadily the phenomena escalated to include: knives, coins and other objects being thrown, mysterious messages appearing on a child's 'doodle board' and bizarre lights floating in and out of solid objects.

978 07509 4874 6

Haunted Leeds
KENNETH GOOR

From creepy accounts of the city centre and surrounding suburbs to phantoms of the theatre, haunted hotels and pubs, *Haunted Leeds* contains a chilling range of ghostly goings-on. Drawing on historical and contemporary sources, you will hear about the ex-librarian who haunts Leeds Library, the ghost of a murderer at the Town Hall, Mary Bateman the Leeds Witch, as well as many other spectral monks, soldiers and white ladies!

978 07524 4016 3

Ghost-Hunter's Casebook
BOWEN PEARSE

This is an essential guide to the career of Britain's most eminent ghost hunter, Andrew Green, who investigated hundreds of hauntings during his career. The most important cases from his lifetime of research – each of which has been extensively re-researched and updated by Bowen Pearse, who knew Andrew for many years, and who has complete access to all of his personal papers – are collected together in this volume.

978 07524 4500 7

If you are interested in purchasing other books published by The History Press, or in case you have difficulty finding any History Press books in your local bookshop, you can also place orders directly through our website
www.thehistorypress.co.uk